# The Emerging Fourth Generation of Chinese Investment Treaties

Junqing Chao

# The Emerging Fourth Generation of Chinese Investment Treaties

## Progress, Prospects and Implications

Springer

Junqing Chao
Shenzhen, Guangdong, China

ISBN 978-981-95-5051-7 ISBN 978-981-95-5052-4 (eBook)
https://doi.org/10.1007/978-981-95-5052-4



This Springer imprint is published by the registered company Springer Nature Singapore Pte Ltd.
The registered company address is: 152 Beach Road, #21-01/04 Gateway East, Singapore 189721, Singapore

**Acknowledgements** This book builds upon my doctoral thesis and practical experience in arbitration. Back in 2019, when I graduated, the international investment law regime was undergoing a profound transformation, while China's domestic investment reforms were progressing at a rapid pace. Many issues surrounding China's fourth-generation investment treaties remained unresolved. Yet over the past five years, China has concluded significant investment treaties, completed its domestic investment reforms, and actively engaged in investment treaty arbitration. These developments mark significant breakthroughs in the evolution of its fourth-generation investment treaties. Having witnessed these changes firsthand, I have felt compelled to revisit this topic. I believe this discussion will be valuable not only to Chinese scholars and practitioners working on investment treaties and arbitration, but also to their international counterparts seeking to understand China's domestic investment reforms and their interactions with investment treaties.

My deepest gratitude goes to my supervisor, Professor Chin Leng Lim. He inspired me to begin this research and entrusted me with the freedom to pursue it. It was also he who encouraged me to step into the world of arbitration—a journey for which I am endlessly thankful. This invaluable experience has not only equipped me with practical skills but also provided new perspectives that profoundly enriched my theoretical work. I am also deeply grateful to Professor Hualing Fu and Professor Yun Zhao for their consistent support and encouragement along the way. My sincere thanks go to Professor Muthucumaraswamy Sornarajah and Professor Xianchu Zhang for their insightful and valuable feedback on my doctoral thesis. I would also like to extend my appreciation to the Springer team for their kindness and assistance in preparing this book. Lastly, I wish to deeply thank my parents for their endless love and selfless support—I am forever indebted to them. As I concluded in the acknowledgments of my doctoral thesis, this book is not a destination, but part of a wonderful journey.

**Competing Interests** The author has no competing interests to declare that are relevant to the content of this manuscript.

# Contents

# About the Author

**Dr. Junqing Chao** obtained her Ph.D. from the University of Hong Kong. Her research focused on international law and arbitration, and her work was presented in Paris, Bern and Hong Kong. After graduation, she worked at King & Wood Mallesons, where she specialized in international commercial and investment arbitration. She has represented and assisted clients in arbitration proceedings under a range of arbitration rules, including those of the ICC, SIAC, HKIAC, AAA/ICDR, CIETAC, SAIC, and UNCITRAL. She has also served as an arbitrator for several international moot competitions, including the FDI Moot Shenzhen, FDI Moot Vietnam, and the Frankfurt Investment Arbitration Moot Court.

# Abbreviations

| | |
|---|---|
| ASEAN | Association of Southeast Asian Nations |
| BIT | Bilateral Investment Treaty |
| BRI | Belt and Road Initiative |
| CAI | China-EU Comprehensive Agreement on Investment |
| CETA | EU-Canada Comprehensive Economic and Trade Agreement |
| CJVL | Chinese-Foreign Contractual Joint Ventures Law |
| CPTPP | Comprehensive and Progressive Agreement for Trans-Pacific Partnership |
| ECT | Energy Charter Treaty |
| EJVL | Chinese-Foreign Equity Joint Ventures Law |
| EU | European Union |
| FCN | Friendship, Commerce, and Navigation |
| FDI | Foreign Direct Investment |
| FET | Fair and Equitable Treatment |
| FIE | Foreign-Invested Enterprise |
| FIFD | Friends of Investment Facilitation for Development |
| FPS | Full Protection and Security |
| FTA | Free Trade Agreement |
| FTC | Free Trade Commission |
| FTZ | Free Trade Zone |
| G20 Guiding Principles | G20 Guiding Principles for Global Investment Policymaking |
| GATS | General Agreement on Trade in Services |
| ICS | Investment Court System |
| ICSID | International Centre for Settlement of Investment Disputes |
| IFD Agreement | Investment Facilitation for Development Agreement |
| IIA | International Investment Agreement |
| ISDS | Investor-State Dispute Settlement |
| MAI | Multilateral Agreement on Investment |

| | |
|---|---|
| MFN | Most-Favored-Nation |
| MIC | Multilateral Investment Court |
| NAFTA | North American Free Trade Agreement |
| OECD | Organization for Economic Co-operation and Development |
| OFDI | Outward Foreign Direct Investment |
| RCEP | Regional Comprehensive Economic Partnership |
| SAR | Special Administrative Region |
| SOE | State-Owned Enterprise |
| TIPs | Treaties with Investment Provisions |
| TIT | Trilateral Investment Agreement |
| TRIMS | Agreement on Trade-Related Investment Measures |
| TTIP | Transatlantic Trade and Investment Partnership |
| UNCITRAL | United Nations Commission on International Trade Law |
| UNCTAD | United Nations Conference on Trade and Development |
| US | United States |
| USMCA | United States-Mexico-Canada Agreement |
| VCLT | Vienna Convention on the Law of Treaties |
| WFEL | Wholly Foreign-Owned Enterprise Law |
| WTO | World Trade Organization |

# Chapter 1
# Introduction

This chapter serves as the introduction to the book. It first examines the existing scholarship on Chinese investment treaties and, more specifically, on their fourth generation (Sects. 1.1 through 1.3), before introducing the book's key questions and central themes (Sect. 1.4). The chapter concludes with an outline of the subsequent chapters (Sect. 1.5).

## 1.1 Why Chinese Investment Treaties?

In 1978, China adopted the "Open Door" policy, aiming to attract foreign investment to promote its economic development. To achieve this goal, domestically, China enacted the Law on Chinese-Foreign Equity Joint Ventures (EJVL) in 1979, allowing foreign companies to establish joint ventures with Chinese entities. Internationally, China launched the bilateral investment treaty (BIT) program in 1982, providing foreign investors with legal assurance and confidence [1]. As a result, China's foreign direct investment (FDI) inflows saw a significant increase.

In 1998, China introduced the Going Global Strategy to encourage domestic companies to invest abroad. Following its accession to the World Trade Organization (WTO) in 2001, China incorporated this strategy into its Tenth Five-Year Plan (2001–2005) and simplified the approval procedurals for outward foreign direct investment (OFDI) projects [1–4]. Concurrently, China expanded its BIT network with both developed and developing countries, further strengthening legal protection for investors [1]. These measures collectively contributed to a significant rise in China's OFDI flows.

Today, China has emerged as a major player in international investment flows. According to the United Nations Conference on Trade and Development (UNCTAD), China consistently ranked among the top five economies for both FDI and OFDI between 2022 and 2024 [5–7]. A significant milestone was reached in 2024 when

 
J. Chao, *The Emerging Fourth Generation of Chinese Investment Treaties*,
https://doi.org/10.1007/978-981-95-5052-4_1

China's OFDI (163 billion dollars) surpassed its FDI (116 billion dollars), making it a net capital exporter [7]. Furthermore, China has developed a comprehensive network of investment treaties, with 109 BITs and 30 treaties with investment provisions (TIPs)—collectively referred to as international investment agreements (IIAs)—currently in force [8]. Especially in recent years, China has actively negotiated and concluded investment treaties with major economies, such as the United States (US), the European Union (EU), Canada, Australia, Japan, Korea, and the Association of Southeast Asian Nations (ASEAN).

Given China's growing influence, its investment treaties have become a critically important subject in the field of international investment law, warranting in-depth study and attention.

## 1.2 Research on Chinese Investment Treaties

In the existing literature on Chinese investment treaties, one of the most important works is a monograph *Chinese Investment Treaties: Policies and Practice,* authored by Gallagher and Shan and published in 2009 [1]. This monograph represents a milestone in the scholarship on Chinese investment treaties.

Prior to 2009, international legal scholarship had paid "little attention" to Chinese investment treaties, despite their fundamental shift from a conservative to a liberal approach in 1998 [9]. Only several writings, primarily in the form of journal articles or book chapters, briefly introduced the evolution of Chinese investment treaties [10–12]. However, Chinese scholars engaged in an intense debate regarding this liberal approach. In 2007, Chen, a prominent Chinese scholar, edited and published a book (in Chinese) that critically examined China's liberal BIT stance. Two chapters of this book were subsequently published in a specialized international journal (in English) [13–15].

In 2009, Gallagher and Shan in their monograph conducted a comprehensive and systematic examination of China's investment treaty policies and practice. Based on the three versions of Chinese Model BIT,[1] Chinese investment treaties were categorized into three generations: the first generation (1982–1989), the second generation (1990–1997) and the third generation (1998 to the date of publication) [1]. The liberal approach mentioned above was adopted by the third generation of Chinese investment treaties, while the first and second generations exhibited a conservative approach, especially concerning national treatment and investor-state dispute settlement (ISDS) provisions. Furthermore, Gallagher and Shan responded to criticisms

[1] The three versions of Chinese Model BIT were documented in the annexes of Gallagher and Shan's monograph. According to their research, these three versions were obtained from the Directorate-General of Treaty and Law of China's Ministry of Commerce and were adopted in approximately 1984, 1989 and 1997 respectively. Furthermore, World Trade Institute has documented a China Model BIT (2009). However, this 2009 Model BIT should not be considered as the fourth version of Chinese Model BIT, because subsequent Chinese investment treaties have undergone substantial modifications.

regarding China's liberal BIT approach by proposing a New Model BIT designed to balance the rights and obligations between host states and foreign investors [1].

It should be emphasized that Gallagher and Shan's classification constitutes an academic framework, designed to systematically examine the evolution of Chinese investment treaties. Within the existing scholarship, some scholars alternatively categorized pre-1998 Chinese investment treaties as the first generation (marked by conservative features) and post-1998 Chinese investment treaties as the second generation (reflecting a liberal stance) [9]. Since Gallagher and Shan's three-generation framework has gained predominant acceptance in the field, this book will accordingly build upon their framework to analyze the emerging fourth generation of Chinese investment treaties.

After 2009, scholarly attention to Chinese investment treaties has significantly increased, with research focusing primarily on the following issues:

(1) Scholars have specifically examined the key provisions of Chinese investment treaties, such as national treatment, ISDS, expropriation and environmental protection [16–19]. Their analysis covers newly concluded investment treaties, such as the 2009 China-ASEAN investment agreement, 2012 China-Canada BIT, 2012 China-Japan-Korea Trilateral Investment Agreement (TIT), 2020 Regional Comprehensive Economic Partnership (RCEP) and 2020 China-EU Comprehensive Agreement on Investment (CAI)[2] [20–24], as well as significant treaty negotiations, including the China-US BIT negotiations [25, 26].

(2) *Tza Yap Shum v. Peru*, the first investment arbitration case initialed under Chinese investment treaties, has generated significant interest in China's practice in investment treaty arbitration [27]. Early scholarship examined the evolution of China's ISDS provisions, the enforcement of investment arbitral awards in China, and the reasons for the limited number of cases filed under Chinese investment treaties despite their large volume [28, 29]. With the conclusion of *Tza Yap Shum v. Peru* and other cases, scholarly attention shifted toward case analyses [30–33]. Criticisms primarily concern two key issues: the interpretation of restrictive ISDS provisions in Chinese investment treaties and the applicability of Chinese investment treaties to the Hong Kong and Macao Special Administrative Regions (SARs). To date, 28 cases have been initialed under Chinese investment treaties, with 20 brought by Chinese investors and 8 filed against the Chinese government [34].

(3) Scholars have also examined China's investment treaty policy and practice within a broader context, including the availability and effectiveness of Chinese investment treaties under the Belt and Road Initiative (BRI) as well as China's ISDS reform proposal submitted to the United Nations Commission on International Trade Law (UNCITRAL) [35–37]. Furthermore, scholars have assessed China's influence on and contributions to international investment law, with a

[2] It should be noted that the 2020 CAI were concluded in principle, representing an initial step in the process. The CAI primarily focuses on investment liberalization, while investment protection and dispute settlement mechanism remain subject to further negotiations between China and the EU.

particular focus on evaluating whether China continues to act primarily as a rule-taker or has emerged as a rule-maker [38, 39].

## 1.3 Research on the Fourth Generation of Chinese Investment Treaties

In the scholarship, scholar have identified two distinctive features in the post-2008 Chinese investment treaties. First, departing from the liberal approach of the third generation, Chinese investment treaties have started to adopt a balanced approach to investment protection, aiming to recalibrate the relationship between protecting foreign investors and preserving the regulatory space of host states [40]. This balanced approach is not unique to China. Amid the current global backlash against investment arbitration, numerous countries, including the US and the EU, have been upgrading their investment treaties to preserve more regulatory space for host states [41, 42]. It has also been observed that China's balancing practice has drawn lessons from the US experience, especially the 2004 US Model BIT [40].

Second, beyond investment protection, Chinese investment treaties have incorporated an additional theme: investment liberalization—an aspect entirely unaddressed in the first three generations. The core provisions of investment liberalization are the pre-establishment national treatment and negative list approach. After accepting these requirements at the investment treaty level, China has undertaken domestic investment reforms. In 2019, China enacted a new Foreign Investment Law (New Foreign Investment Law), establishing a more open and liberalized foreign investment regulatory regime [43].

In light of these developments, during the period from 2015 to 2019, several scholars, based on the balanced investment protection approach and/or the newly introduced investment liberalization provisions, argued that the fourth generation of Chinese investment treaties was emerging [44–46].

However, it is important to emphasize two key points. First, these two features together serve as defining characteristics of China's fourth-generation investment treaties, distinguishing them from the first three generations. Specifically, the fourth generation of Chinese investment treaties, emerging post-2008, is built on two fundamental pillars: (1) the promotion of investment liberalization; and (2) the balance of investment protection with the right of states to regulate. The key characteristics of these generational shifts can be summarized as follows (Table 1.1).

**Table 1.1** Key Characteristics of China's Four Generations of Investment Treaties

| | 1st G | 2nd G | 3rd G | 4th G |
|---|---|---|---|---|
| Period | 1982–1989 | 1990–1997 | 1998–2007 | 2008-present |
| Protection | Conservative | Conservative | Liberal | Balanced |
| Liberalization | Not Addressed | | | Liberal |

Second, the development of these two features remains ongoing. Especially since 2019, China's investment treaty practice and arbitration have witnessed several landmark developments, including (1) the submission of its ISDS reform proposal to UNCITRAL in 2019 [47]; (2) the conclusion of two significant investment treaties in 2020—the RCEP with ASEAN, Australia, Japan, Korea, and New Zealand as well as the CAI with the EU [48, 49]; (3) the publication of the implementing regulations for the New Foreign Investment Law in 2019, further refining China's foreign investment regulatory regime [50]; and (4) a surge in China's investment arbitration cases, with 18 cases filed between 2019 and 2024 (compared to simply 10 cases in total from 2007 to 2018) [34].

These developments demonstrate China's continued efforts to balance investment protection with the right of states to regulate while advancing investment liberalization through comprehensive treaty commitments. This evolutionary process explains the title of this book—the *emerging* fourth generation of Chinese investment treaties. Given these recent significant developments, now is an opportune time to conduct a comprehensive and systematic analysis of this fourth generation of Chinese investment treaties.

## 1.4 Questions and Themes

Given its purpose, this book mainly addresses the following three questions:

(1) To what extent have the post-2008 Chinese investment treaties promoted investment liberalization and balanced investment protection with the right of states to regulate?

(2) What possible approaches could the future Chinese investment treaties adopt to address the remaining challenges in the fourth generation's development?

(3) What implications does the fourth generation of Chinese investment treaties have for international investment law, particularly in relation to the ongoing reform of the investment treaty regime?

The examination of these questions corresponds to this book's three themes: progress, prospects and implications. Regarding these themes, three critical points warrant clarification. First, the evolutionary process of China's fourth-generation investment treaties differs fundamentally from that of preceding generations. The evolution of the first three generations essentially represented a gradual acceptance of the then-prevailing liberal BIT approach—characterized by broad investment protection provisions. Each generational shift occurred at identifiable junctures: the transition from the first to the second generation was triggered by China's accession to the International Centre for Settlement of Investment Disputes (ICSID) Convention in 1990, while the shift from the second to the third generation resulted from China's adoption of the Going Global Strategy in 1998 and its full embrace of the liberal BIT approach [1]. In contrast, the fourth generation follows a process of progressive evolution—one that began in 2008 and remains ongoing to this day. Notably, many significant breakthroughs have been achieved only in the past five years. Moreover, some critical issues still await resolution and require further development.

Second, the progressive evolution of China's fourth-generation investment treaties has been driven by multiple factors. At the international level, international investment law has faced a legitimacy crisis over the past two decades, with criticisms primarily focusing on arbitral tribunals' expansive interpretations of treaty provisions. Beginning with the North American Free Trade Agreement (NAFTA), the backlash against investment arbitration has spread globally [51]. As noted above, numerous countries, including the US and the EU, have been upgrading their investment treaties to strike a balance between investment protection and the right of states to regulate [52]. This balancing debate remains ongoing and has even intensified.

Additionally, the scope and objectives of investment treaties have expanded to incorporate not only investment protection but also investment liberalization. The US has championed this approach, as evidenced by its 2004 and 2012 Model BITs [41, 53]. Today, the EU has taken this approach even further, advancing investment liberalization in a more comprehensive manner [42]. Furthermore, with the negotiation and finalization of the WTO Investment Facilitation for Development Agreement (IFD Agreement), an increasing number of investment treaties have begun to address investment facilitation [54]. Unlike investment liberalization (focusing on opening markets), investment facilitation emphasizes reducing barriers and streamlining procedures, making it more widely acceptable to states [54, 55].

At the domestic level, China itself has been undergoing significant changes. For example, as discussed, China has established a completely new and open foreign investment regulatory regime under the New Foreign Investment Law [43]. In addition, the increasing number of investment arbitration cases has put Chinese investment treaties to the test, raising questions about how their provisions will be interpreted, whether such interpretations will be consistent with the intentions of the contracting parties, and how they will likely influence China's future investment treaty practice. Furthermore, China's dual role as both a capital importer and a capital exporter will undoubtedly impact its approach to investment treaties. With an increasing number of Chinese companies investing abroad under the BRI, China is expected to pay greater attention to protecting its OFDI interests.

Third, China's fourth-generation investment treaties hold considerable significance. Internationally, these treaties reflect China's stance on and possible contributions to the ongoing reform of the investment treaty regime. Given the scale of China's FDI and OFDI, its position warrants attention. Domestically, these treaties are helping to liberalize its investment market—a development closely watched by foreign investors. At the same time, as Chinese companies expand overseas, they are increasingly interested in how these treaties can protect their investments abroad.

In light of this, research on China's fourth-generation investment treaties requires not only linking them to domestic political, economic, and legal developments but also examining them within the broader context of international investment law.

## 1.5 Outline of Chapters

The book comprises eight chapters. Following this introductory chapter, Chapters 2 through 5 collectively explore the key features and driving forces behind China's fourth-generation investment treaties, while Chapters 6 and 7 evaluate their broader implications for international investment law. Chapter 8 concludes the book. More specifically:

Chapter 2 focuses on the investment liberalization provisions in China's fourth-generation investment treaties. It first traces China's historically restrictive approach to investment liberalization, as reflected in its first three generations of investment treaties and its former foreign investment regulatory regime. Then, it examines the shift in China's policy stance, particularly through the reforms in the Shanghai Free Trade Zone (FTZ) and the enactment of the New Foreign Investment Law. Finally, against the backdrop of China's newly established open and liberalized foreign investment regulatory regime, the chapter assesses its current treaty commitments to investment liberalization within its fourth-generation investment treaties.

Chapter 3 focuses on the substantive standards of investment protection in China's fourth-generation investment treaties. It begins by introducing the broader context of ongoing investment treaty reforms. Next, it systematically traces the evolution of China's approach to substantive investment protection across the first three generations before analyzing the fourth generation. The analysis focuses on five key substantive provisions: (1) definitions of investment and investor; (2) national treatment and Most-favored-nation (MFN) treatment; (3) fair and equitable treatment (FET) and full protection and security (FPS); (4) indirect expropriation; and (5) exception clauses. The chapter also examines how arbitral tribunals have interpreted the first three generations of treaties and discusses the implications of these interpretations for China's fourth-generation investment treaty practice.

Chapter 4 focuses on the ISDS provisions in China's fourth-generation investment treaties. It begins by introducing the global backlash against investment arbitration and corresponding ISDS reform efforts. Next, it examines the evolution and interpretation of the ISDS provisions across the first three generations of investment treaties, highlighting two critical issues in arbitral practice: (1) the conflicting interpretations of restrictive ISDS provisions and (2) the application of Chinese investment treaties to the Hong Kong and Macao SARs. Finally, the chapter examines the extent to which China's fourth-generation investment treaties have refined the ISDS provisions, discusses persistent challenges in reforming the ISDS mechanism, and explores potential solutions to address these challenges.

Chapter 5 summarizes the key features of China's fourth-generation investment treaties and analyzes the five major factors driving their development. These factors include (1) the changing landscape of international investment treaties; (2) the need to balance investment protection with the right of states to regulate; (3) the fundamental reform of China's foreign investment regulatory regime; (4) China's growing ODFI and evolving role in international law; and (5) China's increasing involvement in investment treaty arbitration. The chapter argues that these fourth-generation treaties reflect a liberal approach to investment liberalization and a balanced approach to investment protection. It further argues that, through these four generations of treaties, China has established a comprehensive investment treaty network at the bilateral, regional and multilateral levels.

Chapter 6 examines recent trends and developments in international investment law, addressing both the global backlash against investment arbitration and the ongoing investment treaty reforms. The analysis focuses on reforms at multiple levels: (1) nationally, through the balancing approaches adopted by the US, the EU, and India in their recent investment treaties; (2) bilaterally and regionally, through the negotiation and conclusion of recent investment treaties, particularly mega-regional agreements such as the Comprehensive and Progressive Agreement for Trans-Pacific Partnership (CPTPP) and RCEP; and (3) multilaterally, through the reform efforts undertaken at the UNCITRAL, ICSID, Organization for Economic Co-operation and Development (OECD) and WTO. The chapter concludes with a comprehensive assessment of the current landscape of investment treaty reform.

Chapter 7 analyzes the broader implications of China's fourth-generation investment treaties for the ongoing investment treaty reforms. Building upon the multi-level reform framework, the chapter seeks to address three key questions: (1) how China's fourth-generation investment treaties constitute an emerging model in the balancing debate at the national level; (2) how China has pursed rule consolidation through treaty negotiations at the bilateral and regional levels; and (3) how China has actively participated in multilateral investment rulemaking. Based on this analysis, the chapter finally evaluates China's evolving role in international investment governance.

Chapter 8 serves as the book's conclusion, synthesizing its findings through two aspects: (1) the key features of and driving forces behind China's fourth-generation investment treaties; and (2) the contributions of these treaties in addressing the global backlash against investment arbitration and the ongoing investment treaty reforms.

Overall, this book offers a comprehensive and systematic analysis of China's fourth-generation investment treaties and their broader implications for international investment law.

## References


1. Norah Gallagher and Wenhua Shan. (2009). Chinese Investment Treaties: Policies and Practice. Oxford: OUP
2. Outline of the 10th Five-Year Plan (2001–2005) for the National Economic and Social Development of the People's Republic of China (2001)
3. Interim Measures for the Administration of Examination and Approval of the Overseas Investment Projects (2004)
4. Provisions on the Examination and Approval of Investment to Run Enterprises Abroad (2004)
5. UNCTAD (2023) World Investment Report 2023: Investing in Sustainable Energy for All. Switzerland
6. UNCTAD (2024) World Investment Report 2024: Investment Facilitation and Digital Government. Switzerland

7. UNCTAD (2025) World Investment Report 2025: International Investment in the Digital Economy. Switzerland
8. UNCTAD, International Investment Agreements Navigator: China. https://investmentpolicy.unctad.org/international-investment-agreements/countries/42/china. Accessed 23 August 2025
9. Stephen W. Schill (2007) Tearing Down the Great Wall: The New Generation Investment Treaties of the People's Republic of China. Cardozo Journal of International and Comparative Law, Volume 15, Issue 1: 73-115
10. Shishi Li (1988) Bilateral Investment Promotion and Protection Agreements: Practice of the People's Republic of China. In: Paul de Waart, Paul Peters and Erik Denters (ed) International Law and Development. Nijhoff, p 163-184
11. Qingjiang Kong (1998–1999) Bilateral Investment Treaties: The Chinese Approach and Practice. Asian Yearbook of International Law, Volume 8: 105–136
12. Peter Turner and Mark Mangan (2007) Substantive and Procedural Rights under China's Investment Treaties. Asian Counsel, Volume 5, Issue 4: 39
13. An Chen and Congyan Cai (eds) (2007) New Development in International Investment Law and New Practice of China's Bilateral Investment Treaties (in Chinese: Guo Ji Tou Zi Fa De Xin Fa Zhan Yu Zhong Guo Shuang Bian Tou Zi Tiao Yue De Xin Shi Jian). Fudan, Shanghai
14. An Chen (2006) Should the Four Great Safeguards in Sino-Foreign BITs be Hastily Dismantled? Comments on Provisions Concerning Dispute Settlement in Model U.S. and Canadian BIT. Journal of World Investment & Trade, Volume 7, Issue 6: 899–933
15. Congyan Cai (2007) Change of the Structure of International Investment and the Development of Developing Countries' BIT Practice. Journal of World Investment & Trade, Volume 8, Issue 6: 829-847
16. Wenhua Shan, Norah Gallagher and Sheng Zhang (2012) National Treatment for Foreign Investment in China: A Changing Landscape. ICSID Review, Volume 27, Issue 1: 120-144
17. J. Romesh Weeramantry (2012) Investor-State Dispute Settlement Provisions in China's Investment Treaties. ICSID Review, Volume 27, Issue 1: 192-206
18. Ye Ji (2011) Voluntary "Westernization" of the Expropriation Rules in Chinese BITs and Its Implication: An Empirical Study. Journal of World Investment & Trade, Volume 12, Issue 1: 81-99
19. Manjiao Chi (2015) The "Greenization" of Chinese BITs: An Empirical Study of the Environmental Provisions in Chinese BITs and Its Implications for China's Future BIT-Making. Journal of International Economic Law, Volume 18, Issue 3: 511-542
20. Wei Shen (2010) Leaning Towards a More Liberal Stance? An Evaluation of Substantive Provisions Under the New ASEAN-China Investment Agreement in Light of Chinese BIT Jurisprudence. Arbitration International, Volume 26, Issue 4: 549-596
21. Wei Shen (2010) Is This a Great Leap Forward? A Comparative Review of the Investor-State Arbitration Clause in the ASEAN-China Investment Treaty: From BIT Jurisprudential and Practical Perspectives. Journal of International Arbitration, Volume 27, Issue 4: 379-419
22. Gus Van Harten (2014) Canada's non-reciprocal BIT with China: Would the US or Europe Do the Same?. Columbia FDI Perspectives No. 136. https://ccsi.columbia.edu/sites/ccsi.columbia.edu/files/content/docs/publications/No-136-Van-Harten-FINAL.pdf. Accessed 23 August 2025
23. Jaemin Lee (2013) An Important First Stride, but Beware of the Pitfalls: A Critical Analysis of the ISDS Mechanism of the 2012 Korea-China-Japan Trilateral Investment Treaty. Chinese Journal of International Law, Volume 12, Issue 3: 509-541
24. Julien Chaisse and Matthieu Burnay (2022) Introduction – CAI's Contribution to International Investment Law: European, Chinese, and Global Perspectives. The Journal of World Investment & Trade, Volume 23, Issue 4: 497-520
25. Congyan Cai (2009) China-US Negotiations and the Future of Investment Treaty Regime: A Grand Bilateral Bargain with Multilateral Implications. Journal of International Economic Law, Volume 12, Issue 2: 457-506
26. Karl P. Sauvant and Huiping Chen (2012) A China-US Bilateral Investment Treaty: A Template for a Multilateral Framework for Investment?. Columbia FDI Perspectives No.

85. https://ccsi.columbia.edu/sites/ccsi.columbia.edu/files/content/docs/publications/FDI_85.pdf. Accessed 23 August 2025
27. *Tza Yap Shum v Republic of Peru*, ICSID Case No. ARB/07/6.
28. Kim M. Rooney (2007) ICSID and BIT Arbitrations and China. Journal of International Arbitration, Volume 24, Issue 6: 689-712
29. Monika C.E. Heymann (2008) International Law and the Settlement of Investment Disputes Relating to China. Journal of International Economic Law, Volume 11, Issue 3: 507-526
30. An Chen (2009) Queries to the Recent ICSID Decision on Jurisdiction Upon the Case of Tza Yap Shum v. Republic of Peru: Should China-Peru BIT 1994 be Applied to Hong Kong SAR under the "One Country Two systems" Policy?. Journal of World Investment & Trade, Volume 10, Issue 6: 337–372
31. Wei Shen (2011) The Good, the Bad or the Ugly? A Critique of the Decision on Jurisdiction and Competence in Tza Yap Shum v. The Republic of Peru. Chinese Journal of International Law, Volume 10: 55-95
32. Juan Du and Zhenxing Zhang (2024) AsiaPhos Limited and Norwest Chemicals Pte Ltd v People's Republic of China: Unpredictable Jurisdiction under the Restrictive ISDS Mechanism. ICSID Review, Volume 39, Issue 1: 29-41
33. Ming Du (2021) The Status of Chinese State-Owned Enterprises in International Investment Arbitration: Much Ado about Nothing?. Chinese Journal of International Law, Volume 20, Issue 4: 785-815
34. UNCTAD, Investment Dispute Settlement Navigator: China. https://investmentpolicy.unctad.org/investment-dispute-settlement/country/42/china/investor. Accessed 23 August 2025
35. Sornarajah Muthucumaraswamy (2020) Chinese Investment Treaties in the Belt and Road Initiative Area. The Chinese Journal of Comparative Law, Volume 8, Issue 1: 55-78
36. Jamieson M. Kirkwood and Julien Chaisse (2023) Chinese Puzzle: Anatomy of the (Invisible) Belt And Road Investment Treaty. Journal of International Economic Law, Volume 8, Issue 1: 245-269
37. Ming Du (2023) Explaining China's approach to Investor-State Dispute Settlement Reform: A Contextual Perspective. European Law Journal, Volume 28: 281-303
38. Freya Baetens and Sheng Zhang (2024) China: An Emerging Rule-Maker in International Investment Law?. In: Ignacio de la Rasilla and Congyan Cai (ed) The Cambridge Handbook of China and International Law. Cambridge, p 423–449
39. Axel Berger (2023) China's International Investment Agreement Policy: From Rule-Taker to Rule-Maker?. In: Henry Gao, Damian Raess, and Ka Zeng (ed) China and the WTO: a Twenty-Year Assessment. Cambridge, p 452–467
40. Elodie Dulac (2010) The Emerging Third Generation of Chinese Investment Treaties. Transnational Dispute Settlement 4
41. United States Model BIT (2012)
42. EU-Canada Comprehensive Economic and Trade Agreement (2016)
43. Foreign Investment Law of the People's Republic of China (2019)
44. Karl P. Sauvant and Michael D. Nolan (2015) China's Outward Foreign Direct Investment and International Investment Law. Journal of International Economic Law, Volume 18, Issue 4: 893-934
45. Wenhua Shan and Hongrui Chen (2016) China-US BIT Negotiation and the Emerging Chinese BIT 4.0. In: C. L. Lim (ed), Alternative Visions of the International Law on Foreign Investment: Essays in Honour of Muthucumaraswamy Sornarajah. Cambridge, p 223–254
46. Matthew Levine (2019) Towards A Fourth Generation of Chinese Treaty Practice: Substantive Changes, Balancing Mechanisms, And Selective Adaption. In: Julien Chaisse (ed) China's International Investment Strategy: Bilateral, Regional, and Global Law and Policy. Oxford, p 205–221
47. UNCITRAL (2019) A/CN.9/WG.III/WP.177 Possible Reform of Investor-State Dispute Settlement (ISDS): Submission from the Government of China. https://docs.un.org/en/A/CN.9/WG.III/WP.177. Accessed 12 August 2025
48. Regional Comprehensive Economic Partnership (2020)

49. China-EU Comprehensive Agreement on Investment (2020)
50. Regulation for Implementing the Foreign Investment Law of the People's Republic of China (2019)
51. Michael Waibel, Asha Kaushal, Kyo-Hwa Liz Chung and Claire Balchin (eds) (2010) The Backlash against Investment Arbitration. Kluwer, London
52. UNCTAD (2020) International Investment Agreements Reform Accelerator. Switzerland
53. United States Model BIT (2004)
54. Investment Facilitation for Development Agreement (2024)
55. WTO, The Investment Facilitation for Development (IFD) Agreement. https://www.wto.org/english/tratop_e/invfac_public_e/invfac_intro_e.htm. Accessed 23 August 2025

# Chapter 2
# Investment Liberalization

This chapter analyzes the investment liberalization provisions in China's fourth-generation investment treaties. First, it contextualizes the discussion by outlining the promotion and evolution of investment liberalization in investment treaties (Sect. 2.1). Next, it examines China's historically restrictive approach to investment liberalization, as evidenced in its first three generations of investment treaties and its former foreign investment regulatory regime (Sect. 2.2). Subsequently, the chapter analyzes China's evolving policy stance on investment liberalization through two key developments: (1) the establishment of a new, open, and liberalized foreign investment regulatory regime under the New Foreign Investment Law; and (2) the corresponding substantial and comprehensive liberalization commitments in its fourth-generation investment treaties (Sect. 2.3).

## 2.1 The Promotion and Evolution of Investment Liberalization

Investment liberalization used to be considered as a main feature to distinguish the "European Model" BITs (covering only investment protection) from the "US Model" BITs (covering both investment liberalization and investment protection). However, today, investment liberalization has emerged as a key pillar in the EU's international investment policy [1]. The core provision of investment liberalization is market access, or pre-establishment national treatment. This issue is not only a key point in the China-US and China-EU BIT negotiations but also a defining feature of China's fourth-generation investment treaties.

In addition to market access, investment liberalization also concerns other issues, including the prohibition of performance requirements, the promotion of regulatory transparency, the protection of environment and labor rights, and the promotion of



J. Chao, *The Emerging Fourth Generation of Chinese Investment Treaties*,
https://doi.org/10.1007/978-981-95-5052-4_2

corporate social responsibility. Furthermore, the issue of investment facilitation has received increasing attention. These issues will be examined in detail as below.

### 2.1.1 *Market Access*

European countries traditionally viewed BITs as instruments to provide legal protection for foreign investors, while permitting host states to determine the conditions for the admission of investments [2]. Consequently, an "admission clause" was commonly incorporated. For example, the 2005 Germany Model BIT provided that the contracting states shall promote investments and admit them in accordance with their domestic laws and regulations [3].

In contrast, the US has consistently sought to establish a right of admission on a non-discriminatory basis, aiming to promote the free movement of foreign investments [4]. In the 1994, 2004 and 2012 US Model BITs, foreign investors were granted national treatment and MFN treatment in both pre- and post-establishment phases—referred to as the "establishment clause" [5–7]. Vandevelde argued that the US BIT practice was grounded in the principle of investment neutrality—emphasizing that investment flows should be led by the market rather than the government [8].

It is worth noting that the "establishment clause" is not absolute and instead is usually coupled with a list of reservations or exceptions (known as the "negative list approach"). The non-conforming measures provision, along with treaty annexes, list the sectors in which the host state reserves the right to withhold pre-establishment national treatment and MFN treatment, or any existing laws and regulations that are inconsistent with these obligations [2].

The US BIT practice has exerted a substantial influence on mega-free trade agreements (FTAs), including the 2018 United States-Mexico-Canada Agreement (USMCA), 2018 CPTPP, and 2020 RCEP [9–11]. The inclusion of pre-establishment national treatment in these mega-FTAs reflects a growing willingness among countries to open their markets to foreign investors and advance investment liberalization through investment treaties.

Moreover, in recent years, European countries have changed their BIT approach, making investment liberalization a central pillar of the EU's international investment policy [1]. Compared to the US, the EU has expanded the scope of national treatment to include the "maintenance, use, and enjoyment" of investment activities, as in the case of the 2016 EU-Canada Comprehensive Economic and Trade Agreement (CETA) [12]. Furthermore, within the framework of CETA, the EU has promoted an absolute market access obligation. This obligation aims to prohibit states from imposing specific restrictions—such as limitations on the number of enterprise, the value of transactions, or the participation of foreign capital—as well as from mandating particular forms of joint ventures [12].

This practice reflects a core objective of EU's international investment policy—to protect EU investors from discrimination and unfair treatment in foreign markets

[13]. Therefore, the EU currently adopts a stronger stance on market access than the US.

### *2.1.2 Performance Requirement Prohibitions*

In addition to pre-establishment national treatment, the prohibition of performance requirements is another tool adopted by the US to promote the principle of investment neutrality. The 1983 US Model BIT prohibited the requirements on export, local content and other similar issues [14, 15]. The 1994 NAFTA expanded the scope of prohibited performance requirement—seven performance requirements for investment-related activities were prohibited, four of which were further prohibited as conditions of the receipt or continued receipt of advantages [16]. The 1994 NAFTA subsequently had a significant impact on the 2004 US Model BIT [6].

The 2012 US Model BIT introduces a new category regarding the purchase, use of, or preference for a particular technology [7]. The investment chapter of the 2018 CPTPP—building upon the 2012 US Model BIT—adds another new category concerning license contracts, bringing the total number of prohibited performance requirements to nine [10]. Although the 2018 USMCA takes an extremely conservative stance on ISDS provisions, it maintains a liberal approach to investment liberalization. Its performance requirements provision is identical to that in the 2018 CPTPP [9, 10]. In contrast, the EU follows the same framework as the 2012 US Model BIT, prohibiting only eight performance requirements, as seen in the 2016 CETA [7, 12]. This approach is also adopted in the 2020 RCEP [11].

A widely recognized harm of performance requirements is that they can distort international trade [17]. Based on this concern, the WTO Agreement on Trade-Related Investment Measures (TRIMs) was established in 1994 to prohibit measures that were inconsistent with national treatment obligations and general elimination of quantitative restrictions [18]. Some countries have chosen to reaffirm their TRIMs obligations in investment treaties, as exemplified by China in the 2012 China-Canada BIT and ASEAN in the 2012 ASEAN-Australia-New Zealand FTA [19, 20]. Although these countries do not commit themselves to additional prohibited performance requirements, this reaffirmation makes their TRIMs obligations subject to investment arbitration [21]. In practice, a few investment arbitration cases have been brought for breach of performance requirements obligations. Most known cases were filed under NAFTA, such as *Mobil Oil v. Canada* [21, 22].

It is also worth highlighting that these performance requirement provisions apply to all investments (not solely to foreign ones). Vandevelde argued that this broad application stemmed from the trade-distorting effect of performance requirements, and that only through this mechanism could host states be prevented from favoring specific investments, thereby avoiding competitive disadvantages for other investments [23].

### 2.1.3 *Regulatory Transparency*

The US has promoted enhanced regulatory transparency, environmental protection and labor rights in investment treaties, as evidenced by its 2004 and 2012 Model BIT [6, 7]. Vandevelde argued that this practice stemmed from the US intention to harmonize its BITs with FTAs, while simultaneously striving to reinforce the norms of international investment regime [23]. He further explained that FTAs typically aimed to advance market liberalization, and as markets became more liberalized, it became necessary to improve information flows and protect the environment and labor rights [23].

Specifically, the 2004 US Model BIT—building upon the 1994 NAFTA—included two new provisions on regulatory transparency. Article 10 required that investment-related laws and regulations should be made public [6]. This provision was considered a mechanism for fostering the rule of law and, more specifically, for instituting a rule-based investment regime [24]. It is noteworthy that Article 10 was subject to investment arbitration. In practice, few tribunals have found breach of regulatory transparency provisions. Instead, transparency is usually regarded as one of elements for the FET standard [24]. For example, the tribunal in *Metalclad v. Mexico* concluded that Mexico had failed to provide a transparent and predictable investment environment, thereby breaching its FET obligation under NAFTA [24, 25].

Furthermore, Article 11 of the 2004 US Model BIT significantly strengthened regulatory transparency obligations by requiring participation in domestic rule-making [2]. Specifically, foreign investors were allowed to comment on proposed measures, present facts and arguments before administrative actions, and support or defend their positions during the review of administrative decisions [6]. Subsequently, the 2012 US Model BIT went further by specifying procedures for publishing laws and regulations, seeking and responding public comments, and permitting investors to participate in standards-setting processes [7].

The publication of laws and regulations and the exchange of information have long been required, but few countries have promoted participation in domestic rulemaking through investment treaties. This approach is evident in the 2018 CPTPP, which largely followed the 2012 US Model BIT but excluded standard-setting provisions [7, 10]. Moving beyond this, the EU has actively promoted regulatory transparency, aiming to facilitate investment by creating a predictable and transparent environment [13].

### 2.1.4 *Environment, Labor and Corporate Social Responsibility*

Building on the 1994 NAFTA, the 2004 US Model BIT also introduced two new provisions addressing environmental protection and labor rights. Articles 12 and 13 prohibited contracting parties from lowering the standards of environmental protection and labor rights to attract foreign investment [6]. Moreover, an environmental exception was included, stating that host states could not be barred from implementing measures for environmental protection [6]. During the review process for the 2012 US Model BIT, civil society called for binding environmental and labor obligations to align with US FTA practice, but this proposal was ultimately rejected [26, 27].

The way environmental concerns are addressed in investment treaties is not limited to these provisions, but also includes references to the environment in treaty preambles, exclusion of environmental regulatory actions from the scope of indirect expropriation, and so forth [28, 29]. The OECD has found that most recently concluded BITs and TIPs contain environmental references [29]. Compared with environmental provisions, labor rights receive less emphasis in investment treaties. Consequently, some commentators have called for stronger host-state obligations to protect labor rights [30].

As mentioned above, Vandevelde noted that environmental and labor provisions were included by the US to align its BITs with FTAs. However, in recent years, these provisions have increasingly been framed within the broader context of sustainable development in international investment law [31]. The concept of sustainable development has gained wider recognition in investment treaties, as exemplified by the 2012 China-Canada BIT [19]. Similarly, corporate social responsibility has begun to be addressed, as evidence by the 2015 Indian Model BIT, 2016 CETA, and 2018 CPTPP [10, 12, 32]. Studies further indicate that the majority of investment treaties concluded between 2008 and 2013 address these issues [33].

### 2.1.5 *Investment Facilitation*

Investment facilitation has gained increasing attention in recent years. While its development has been primarily advanced within the WTO framework—as exemplified by the 2024 IFD Agreement, which aims to improve the business environment and facilitate daily investment activities [34, 35], this issue has also been increasingly addressed in investment treaties, such as the 2020 RCEP [11].

In short, investment liberalization has been increasingly promoted in international investment treaties, especially those of the US, the EU, Canada, and Japan. The pre-establishment national treatment and negative list approach are the main instruments used to achieve market liberalization for foreign investors. Other related issues addressed in investment treaties include performance requirement prohibitions, regulatory transparency, environmental protection, labor rights, corporate social responsibility, and investment facilitation.

## 2.2 Investment Liberalization Under the First Three Generations of Chinese Investment Treaties

### *2.2.1 China's Previous Treaty Commitments*

China's first three generations of investment treaties, modeled after the European Model, only concentrated on the protection of foreign investment. Consequently, they typically included an admission clause. For example, the 2005 China-Germany BIT provided that each contracting party shall admit investments according to its domestic laws and regulations [36]. Similar provisions were incorporated in all three versions of Chinese Model BIT [37–39]. Moreover, national treatment was granted to foreign investors only in the post-establishment stage.

Behind these limited treaty commitments was the fact that China implemented a relatively restrictive regulatory regime for foreign investment at the time. As discussed in Chap. 1, China adopted its "Open Door" policy in 1978, opening its market to the world and welcoming foreign investment. In 1979, China enacted the EJVL, allowing foreign companies to establish joint ventures with Chinese entities and introducing special rules for their establishment, operation and termination [40]. Against this backdrop, China's first BIT—the 1982 China-Sweden BIT—did not provide for national treatment, and this practice continued until 1985 [41, 42].

From 1985 to 1989 (the later stage of the first generation), Chinese investment treaties began to incorporate national treatment provisions, but these provisions only applied to the post-establishment stage and imposed many restrictions. For example, the 1986 China-UK BIT provided for national treatment to the extent possible and in accordance with domestic laws and regulations [43]. Such a provision was referred to as a "best-effort" clause, which only required compliance "to the extent possible" [42]. Moreover, this "best-effort" obligation was conditional on domestic laws and regulations.

Meanwhile, China enacted the Wholly Foreign-Owned Enterprise Law (WFEL) in 1986 and Chinese-Foreign Contractual Joint Ventures Law (CJVL) in 1988. Together with the EJVL, these three laws—collectively referred to as the "Three Foreign Investment Laws"—established a unique regulatory regime for foreign investment in China [44, 45].[1] They imposed special regulations on the entire lifecycle of foreign-invested enterprises (FIEs), including their establishment, daily operations, and termination. These regulations covered areas such as approval procedures, entity forms, foreign ownership, project amendment, tax benefits, foreign exchange and so forth [46]. It is therefore unsurprising that earlier Chinese investment treaties only granted post-establishment national treatment and also subjected national treatment to domestic laws and regulations. This practice continued in the second generation of Chinese investment treaties [38].

[1] It should be noted that, in addition to the "Three Foreign Investment Laws", China promulgated a substantial body of administrative regulations for the management of foreign investment.

In the third generation, with China adopting a liberal BIT approach, qualified national treatment provisions were introduced. These provisions fell into two categories. The first type, as reflected in the Chinese Model BIT Version III, granted national treatment subject to domestic laws and regulations [39]. The second type subjected national treatment to a grandfather clause for existing non-conforming measures [42]. For example, the 2003 China-Germany BIT stipulated that national treatment shall not apply to existing non-conforming measures, including their continuation or amendment (amendments shall not increase the level of non-conformity). It further emphasized that China committed to taking measures to eliminate these non-conforming measures [36]. Some argued that China's changing attitude towards national treatment could be attributed to its accession to the WTO [47].

Overall, from 1982 to 2007, China's first three generations of investment treaties did not address investment liberalization. During this period, China maintained a cautious approach to foreign investment through its restrictive regulatory regime and limited national treatment commitments.

### *2.2.2 China's Former Foreign Investment Regulatory Regime*

As discussed, China initially adopted a relatively restrictive regulatory regime for foreign investment. Under the "Three Foreign Investment Laws", FIEs were required to obtain governmental approval for their establishment and amendment. Furthermore, foreign investments were subject to the Catalogue of Industries for Guiding Foreign Investment (Guidance Catalogue), first published in 1995 and subsequently revised several times [48]. The Guidance Catalogue classified industries into three categories: "encouraged", "restricted", and "prohibited". Foreign investments in the "encouraged" industries could enjoy various benefits in terms of the entity form, foreign ownership, governmental review, investment incentives and so on. In contrast, foreign investments in the "restricted" industries faced more stringent requirements in these aspects, while the "prohibited" industries were completely not open to foreign investments [48].

China's accession to the WTO in 2001 exerted a considerable effect on its foreign investment regulatory regime. First, in compliance with its commitments under the General Agreement on Trade in Services (GATS), China opened numerous service sectors to foreign investments, ranging from business, finance, construction and culture [49, 50]. Second, in compliance with its TRIMs commitments, China abolished the direct performance requirements in the "Three Foreign Investment Laws" [51, 52]. Apart from the TRIMs, China committed to refraining from imposing the requirements concerning technology transfer or research conduct [51, 52].

Subsequently, China undertook further liberalization of its foreign investment regulatory regime. For example, the Guidance Catalogue was further shortened. In the 2015 version, the number of encouraged industries increased to 349, while the number of restricted and prohibited industries decreased to 38 and 36 respectively

[53]. It is fair to say that China made significant progress in market liberalization for foreign investors. However, these changes—especially those made following China's WTO accession—were considered insufficient [52]. Therefore, many called for a more liberal foreign investment regulatory regime in China [52].

## 2.3 Investment Liberalization Under the Fourth Generation of Chinese Investment Treaties

### *2.3.1 China's Changing Attitude*

In 2008, China commenced BIT negotiations with the US. Given that the hallmark of the US Model BIT was investment liberalization, this became a central issue in the negotiations. A breakthrough came in July 2013, when both states affirmed that their BIT would provide the pre-establishment national treatment on the basis of negative list approach [54]. This landmark commitment signaled a fundamental shift in China's attitude to investment liberalization. Subsequently, in September 2013, China established the Shanghai FTZ as a pilot for implementing related reforms [55, 56]. In 2014, China expanded this model by launching three additional FTZs in Fujian, Guangdong, and Tianjin.

One of the most significant reforms implemented by Shanghai FTZ was replacing the approval system with the recordation system. Under this framework, foreign investors did not need to obtain governmental approvals to establish an enterprise in the Shanghai FTZ—unless their investments fell under the negative list [56]. Instead, they simply need to provide investment information and make undertakings [56]. The recordation authority would conduct regular inspections of these undertakings, and if it were to find that the undertakings were inconsistent with actual circumstances, it would order foreign investors to make corrections [56]. The recordation system also extended to project approvals, which were previously handled by the government [57]. Compared with the approval system, the recordation system significantly relaxed control over foreign investment.

Furthermore, Shanghai FTZ published a negative list in 2013, including 190 special administrative measure for restrictions and prohibitions [58]. The number of special administrative measures subsequently decreased to 139 in the 2014 version of the negative list [59]. In 2015, a negative list was issued for all FTZs, further reducing 17 special administrative measures [60]. Despite these efforts, both the US and the EU contended that these negative lists simply regrouped the existing sectors, and they urged China to shorten the list significantly [61, 62]. The differing views on the length of China's negative list were once one of the core issues for the China-US and China-EU BIT negotiations.

The recordation system and negative list of the Shanghai FTZ were deemed successful and were subsequently adopted nationwide. In September 2016, China amended the "Three Foreign Investment Laws", stipulating that FIEs were simply subject to recordation administration if their establishments did not involve special administrative measures [63]. Subsequently, in October 2016, China promulgated the interim measures for the recordation administration system [64]. These rules provided that after FIEs submitted the information, the recordation authority check whether the information was complete and accurate and whether the matters fell within the scope of the recordation [64]. If these requirements were satisfied, the recordation authority would complete the recordation within three working days [64]. In 2018, China published a national negative list for foreign investment, containing only 48 special administrative measure [65].

Overall, from 2013 to 2018, China implemented a series of reforms to progressively and systematically liberalize its investment market, laying solid groundwork for a new, open and liberalized foreign investment regulatory regime.

### *2.3.2 China's New Foreign Investment Regulatory Regime*

In March 2019, China published the New Foreign Investment Law, aiming to replace the "Three Foreign Investment Laws" and converge its foreign and domestic investment regimes [66, 67]. In the 2019 New Foreign Investment Law, the most distinguishing feature is the explicit adoption of the pre-establishment national treatment and negative list approach [66]. It provides that foreign investors are not allowed to invest in the prohibited sectors and must comply with conditions when investing in the restricted sectors. But for the sectors not included in the list, foreign investment shall be administered under the principle of national treatment [66].

Furthermore, an information reporting system has been established for foreign investment. This system requires FIEs to submit investment-related information, and the information reports fall into four categories: initial reports, modification reports, deregistration reports and annual reports [66, 68]. This system is designed not to restrict foreign investment but to achieve better management. The information reporting system has been widely recognized in international investment treaties. For example, the 2012 US Model BIT, while granting pre-establishment national treatment, allows contracting parties to require foreign investors to provide information for statistical purposes [7].

In addition, a national security review mechanism has been established for foreign investment [66]. The specifics of this mechanism are stipulated in the Measures for the Security Review of Foreign Investment published in 2020 [69]. According to this regulation, the national security review covers two main areas: investments related to national defense security (e.g., arms industry) and those affecting broader national security (e.g., key agricultural products, energy and resources) [69]. This regulation also provides that the review authority must complete a general assessment within 30 working days, and if it finds that national security is or may be affected, a special review is triggered [69].

The 2019 New Foreign Investment Law has received predominant attention, as it establishes a new, open and liberalized foreign investment regulatory regime in China.

This legislation forms part of China's Reform 2.0—a comprehensive domestic reform program compared to the 1978 Open Door policy [70, 71]. Economically, China seeks to implement a unified market access system and ensure equal competition for all types of investment [71]. More importantly, it affirms that the market should play the decisive role in resource allocation [71]. China's Reform 2.0 provides a crucial context for the development of China's fourth-generation investment treaties, the broader implications of which will be analyzed in detail in Chap. 5. The following discussion will first examine China's current treaty commitments on investment liberalization under this new regulatory framework.

### 2.3.3 China's Current Treaty Commitments

Since 2008, building upon the fundamental reform of foreign investment regulatory regime, China has gradually advanced investment liberalization in investment treaties. The following will examine the treaty commitments China has undertaken under the emerging fourth generation.

#### 2.3.3.1 Market Access

As mentioned, China accepted pre-establishment national treatment in 2013 during its BIT negations with the US. Prior to that, however, Chinese investment treaties had begun to grant pre-establishment MFN treatment to foreign investors, as exemplified by the 2012 China-Canada BIT [19]. This means that if China were to accept pre-establishment national treatment in future investment treaties, Canadian investors could potentially enjoy the same treatment by virtue of this MFN provision. Berger argued that China's practice was driven by its treaty partners [72]. However, given that most post-2008 Chinese investment treaties include pre-establishment MFN treatment and that the China-US BIT negotiation began in 2008, it is likely that China had already started considering the acceptance of pre-establishment national treatment around that time [19, 73].

In 2019, China promulgated the New Foreign Investment Law, establishing a new, open and liberalized foreign investment regulatory regime. Against this backdrop, China agreed to include pre-establishment national treatment in both the 2020 RCEP and 2020 CAI, marking a comprehensive advancement in the liberalization of China's investment treaty practice [11, 74].

However, pre-establishment national treatment is far from the ultimate goal of investment liberalization in Chinese investment treaties. The 2020 CAI introduces two key innovations. The first one is an absolute market access obligation. As discussed above, the EU first introduced this clause in the 2016 CETA. This provision commits China to granting EU investors a level of market access that exceeds pre-establishment national treatment. The EU has characterized the CAI as locking in China's market openings over the past two decades while securing further access in many sectors [75].

The second major innovation involves the disciplines on state-owned enterprises (SOEs). The CAI adopts an exceptionally broad definition of SOEs, mainly including (1) enterprises in which a contracting state directly or indirectly owns, controls or has power to appoint or direct; and (2) enterprises which are authorized or established by a contracting state as the sole supplier or purchaser of a good or service [74]. This definition is even broader than that of the CPTPP, which primarily covers the first type of SOEs[10, 74].

The CAI establishes three principles for the operation and regulation of SOEs: (1) subject to non-discriminatory fulfillment of public service mandates, SOEs are required to operate based on commercial considerations; (2) in the event that a contracting state has grounds to believe that its interests are adversely impacted by other state's SOEs, it may request that state to disclose detailed information concerning their operations; (3) regulatory bodies should act independently and impartially in regulating all enterprises, including SOEs [74]. The CPTPP incorporates similar principles, along with additional ones in this area [10, 74]. China already applied to join the CPTPP in 2021. It remains to be seen whether China will make a further commitment in this aspect.

Overall, while SOE disciplines have become a key focus in recent international economic rule making practice, the CAI marks the first time China has addressed SOE regulation in its investment treaties. China's willing and ability to undertake these SOE commitments is closely tied to its ongoing SOE reforms [76].

#### 2.3.3.2 Performance Requirement Prohibitions

China reaffirms its TRIMs obligations in the 2012 China-Canada BIT [19]. As noted, this reaffirmation subjects China's TRIMs obligations to investment arbitration. In addition, the 2012 China-Japan-Korea TIT goes further by prohibiting unreasonable or discriminatory measures related to performance requirements on export or transfer of technology [73].

As discussed, the 2018 CPTPP comprehensively prohibits nine performance requirements, four of which are further barred as conditions for receiving advantages [10]. Similar restrictions can be found in the 2020 RCEP, though the RCEP excludes requirements related to purchasing, using, or preferring a specific technology [11]. However, this exception is addressed in the 2020 CAI, which goes even further prohibiting two new categories: the mandatory location of headquarters and the certain percentage or value of research and development [74]. Moreover, the 2020 CAI also expands the scope of prohibited performance requirements as conditions of receiving advantages from four to six categories [74]. Therefore, China has made substantial and comprehensive commitments on performance requirement prohibitions.

It is also worth noting that, in addition to these treaty commitments, the 2020 CAI explicitly prohibits the contracting parties from interfering with technology transfer [74]. The EU contents that this provision would ensure fair competition for its investors in the Chinese market [75]. In fact, China has moved to prohibit forced technology transfers in recent years. The 2019 New Foreign Investment Law explicitly stipulates that technology cooperation shall be voluntary and based on commercial terms and administrative agencies shall not force such transfers [66]. Therefore, the EU and China share a consensus on this issue.

#### 2.3.3.3 Regulatory Transparency, Environment, Labor and Corporate Social Responsibility

The post-2008 Chinese investment treaties have addressed regulatory transparency, environmental protection, labor rights and corporate social responsibility to varying degrees. This is evident in the transparency provision of the 2012 China-Canada BIT and the transparency and environmental provisions of the 2012 China-Japan-Korea TIT [19, 73]. Notably, the 2020 CAI contains the most comprehensive commitments on these issues.

Specifically, regarding regulatory transparency, the CAI requires the contracting parties to promptly publish relevant laws and regulations and allow interested person to comment on proposed measures prior to their enactment [74]. In addition, the CAI addresses the designation of a contact point to provide information, the management of administrative proceedings, and the review and appeal of administrative actions [74]. In Particular, the CAI allows foreign investors to participate in the standards-setting [74]. Moreover, the CAI seeks to protect environment and labor rights, promote responsible business practice and address climate change[74].

Overall, with the conclusion of the CAI, China has made substantial progress in addressing these concerns. These commitments demonstrate that China underscores the sustainable development of international investment regime.

#### 2.3.3.4 Investment Facilitation

As noted above, investment facilitation has been significantly advanced by the 2024 WTO IFD Agreement. In terms of investment treaties, the 2020 RCEP provides that, in accordance with its domestic laws and regulations, each contracting party shall endeavor to: (1) facilitate investments by creating a favorable environment, streamlining approval procedures, and improving information transparency; (2) assist foreign investors in resolving their complaints with the government amicably; (3) address the recurrent issues faced by foreign investors; and (4) foster the exchange of information and knowledge. It also emphasizes that these investment facilitation provisions are not subject to its dispute resolution mechanism [11].

Overall, these provisions reflect RCEP contracting states' willingness to advance investment facilitation. While the 2020 RCEP covers fewer facilitation issues compared to the 2024 WTO IFD Agreement, these provisions highlight the key priorities of the contracting states at the time of its conclusion. For instance, the emphasis on addressing foreign investors' complaints aligns with China's 2019 New Foreign Investment Law, which introduced a comprehensive complaint mechanism for foreign investors [66]. Consequently, investment facilitation has emerged as a key focus in China's investment treaty practice. China has not only shown a strong interest in this area but has also actively promoted related rules within the international investment regime.

## 2.4 Conclusion

The promotion of investment liberalization has emerged as one of the defining features of China's fourth-generation investment treaties. From 2008 to present, China has continuously experimented with investment market liberalization domestically, ultimately establishing a new, open and liberalized foreign investment regulatory regime, while internationally it has progressively undertaken liberalization commitments in its investment treaties. To date, the scope of investment liberalization provisions in Chinese investment treaties extends well beyond pre-establishment national treatment to include absolute market access obligations, SOE disciplines, performance requirement prohibitions, regulatory transparency, environmental protection, labor rights, corporate social responsibility, as well as investment facilitation. Notably, China has undertaken substantial and comprehensive commitments across all these areas. These treaty commitments demonstrate China's determination to create a fairer, more open, and more transparent investment environment.

## References

1. European Commission, Investment-the pillars. https://trade.ec.europa.eu/access-to-markets/en/content/investment-pillars. Accessed 7 August 2025
2. UNCTAD (2007) Bilateral Investment Treaties 1996–2005: Trends in Investment Rulemaking. Switzerland
3. Germany Model BIT (2005)
4. Patrick Juillard (2009) The Law of International Investment: Can the Imbalanced Be Redressed?. In: Karl P. Sauvant (ed) Yearbook on International Investment Law & Policy 2008–2009, Oxford, p 273–282
5. United States Model BIT (1994)
6. United States Model BIT (2004)
7. United States Model BIT (2012)
8. Kenneth J. Vandevelde (2016) The Liberal Vision of the International Law on Foreign Investment. In: C. L. Lim (ed), Alternative Visions of the International Law on Foreign Investment: Essays in Honour of Muthucumaraswamy Sornarajah. Cambridge, p 43–68
9. United States-Mexico-Canada Agreement (2018)
10. Comprehensive and Progressive Agreement for Trans-Pacific Partnership (2018)
11. Regional Comprehensive Economic Partnership (2020)
12. EU-Canada Comprehensive Economic and Trade Agreement (2016)

13. European Commission, Investment. https://policy.trade.ec.europa.eu/help-exporters-and-importers/accessing-markets/investment_en. Accessed 7 August 2025
14. United States Model BIT (1983)
15. Kenneth J. Vandevelde (2009) U.S. International Investment Agreements. Oxford
16. North American Free Trade Agreement (1994)
17. Muthucumaraswamy Sornarajah (2010) The International Law on Foreign Investment. 3rd edn. Cambridge
18. Agreement on Trade-Related Investment Measures (1994)
19. China-Canada BIT (2012)
20. ASEAN-Australia-New Zealand FTA (2012)
21. Suzy H. Nikiema (2014) Performance Requirements in Investment Treaties. IISD Best Practices Series. https://www.iisd.org/sites/default/files/publications/best-practices-performance-requirements-investment-treaties-en.pdf. Accessed 7 August 2025
22. Mobil Investments Canada Inc. and Murphy Oil Corporation v. Canada, ICSID Case No. ARB(AF)/07/4
23. Kenneth. J. Vandevelde (2009) A Comparison of the 2004 and 1994 U.S. Model BITs: Rebalancing Investor and Host Country Interests. In: Karl. P. Sauvant (ed), Yearbook on International Investment Law & Policy 2008–2009. Oxford, p 283–316
24. Kenneth. J. Vandevelde (2010) Bilateral Investment Treaties: History, Policy, and Interpretation. Oxford
25. Metalclad Corporation v. The United Mexican States, ICSID Case No. ARB(AF)/97/1
26. Mark Kantor (2012) Little Has Changed in the New US Model Bilateral Investment Treaty. ICSID Review - Foreign Investment Law Journal, Volume 27, Issue 2: 335-378
27. Paolo Di Rosa and Dawn Y. Yamane Hewett (2013) The New 2012 U.S. Model BIT: Staying the Course. In: Karl P. Sauvant (ed), Yearbook on International Investment Law & Policy 2012–2013. Oxford, p 595–608
28. Kathryn Gordon and Joachim Pohl (2011) Environmental Concerns in International Investment Agreements: The "New Era" Has Commenced, But Harmonization Remains Far Off. Columbia FDI Perspective No. 44. https://ccsi.columbia.edu/sites/ccsi.columbia.edu/files/content/docs/publications/FDI_44.pdf. Accessed 7 August 2025
29. OECD (2011) Environmental Concerns in International Investment Agreements: A Survey. Paris
30. Vid Prislan and Ruben Zanvilet (2013) Labor Provisions in Bilateral Investment Treaties: Does the New US Model BIT Provide a Template for the Future. Columbia FDI Perspective No. 92. https://ccsi.columbia.edu/sites/ccsi.columbia.edu/files/content/docs/publications/FDI_92.pdf. Accessed 7 August 2025
31. UNCTAD (2012) World Investment Report 2012: Towards A New Generation of Investment Policies. Switzerland
32. India Model BIT (2015)
33. Kathryn Gordon, Joachim Pohl and Marie Bouchard (2015) Investment Treaty Law, Sustainable Development and Responsible Business Conduct: A Fact-finding Survey. Columbia FDI Perspective No. 157. https://ccsi.columbia.edu/sites/ccsi.columbia.edu/files/content/docs/publications/No-157-Gordon-Pohl-and-Bouchard-FINAL.pdf. Accessed 7 August 2025
34. The WTO Investment Facilitation for Development Agreement (2024)
35. WTO, The Investment Facilitation for Development (IFD) Agreement. https://www.wto.org/english/tratop_e/invfac_public_e/invfac_intro_e.htm. Accessed 7 August 2025
36. China-Germany BIT (2003)
37. Chinese Model BIT Version I (1984)
38. Chinese Model BIT Version II (1989)
39. Chinese Model BIT Version III (1997)
40. Law of the People's Republic of China on Chinese-Foreign Equity Joint Ventures (1979)
41. China-Sweden BIT (1982)
42. Norah Gallagher and Wenhua Shan (2009) Chinese Investment Treaties: Policies and Practice. Oxford

43. China-UK BIT (1986)
44. Law of the People's Republic of China on Foreign-Capital Enterprises (1986)
45. Law of the People's Republic of China on Chinese-Foreign Contractual Joint Ventures (1988)
46. Vivienne Bath (2011) The Quandary for Chinese Regulatory: Controlling the Flow of Investment into and Out of China. In: Vivienne Bath and Luke Nottage (ed) Foreign Investment and Dispute Resolution Law and Practice in Asia. Routledge, London and New York
47. Karl P. Sauvant and Michael D. Nolan (2015) China's Outward Foreign Direct Investment and International Investment Law. Journal of International Economic Law, Volume 18, Issue 4: 893-934
48. Catalogue of Industries for Guiding Foreign Investment (1995)
49. OECD (2003) OECD Investment Policy Reviews China: Progress and Reform Challenges. Paris
50. WTO (2002), The People's Republic of China, Schedule of Specific Commitments, GATS/SC/135. https://docs.wto.org/dol2fe/Pages/FE_Search/FE_S_S009-DP.aspx?language=E&CatalogueIdList=304181,304174,71613,11725,21775,25776,34016&CurrentCatalogueIdIndex=4&FullTextHash=&HasEnglishRecord=True&HasFrenchRecord=True&HasSpanishRecord=True. Accessed 7 August 2025
51. Julia Ya Qin (2007) Trade, Investment and Beyond: The Impact of WTO Accession on China's Legal System. The China Quarterly No. 191: 720–741
52. Wenhua Shan (2002) Towards a Level Playing Field of Foreign Investment in China. The Journal of World Investment & Trade, Volume 3, Issue 2: 327-343
53. Catalogue of Industries for Guiding Foreign Investment (2015)
54. U.S. Department of the Treasury (2013) Joint U.S.-China Economic Track Fact Sheet of the Fifth Meeting of the U.S.-China Strategic and Economic Dialogue. https://home.treasury.gov/news/press-releases/jl2010Accessed 7 August 2025. Accessed 7 August 2025
55. Jie Huang (2015) Challenges and Solutions for the China-US BIT Negotiations: Insights from the Recent Development of FTZs in China. Journal of International Economic Law, Volume 18, Issue 2: 307-339
56. Notice of the Shanghai Municipal People's Government on Issuing the Measures for the Recordation Administration of Foreign-Funded Enterprises in China (Shanghai) Pilot Free Trade Zone (2013)
57. Notice of the Shanghai Municipal People's Government on Issuing the Measures for the Recordation Administration of Foreign-Funded Projects in China (Shanghai) Pilot Free Trade Zone (2013)
58. Announcement of the Shanghai Municipal People's Government on Issuing the Special Management Measures (Negative List) for Foreign Investment in China (Shanghai) Pilot Free Trade Zone (2013)
59. Special Management Measures (Negative List) for Access of Foreign Investment to China (Shanghai) Pilot Free Trade Zone (2014 Revision)
60. Notice of the General Office of the State Council on Issuing the Special Management Measures (Negative List) for Foreign Investment Access in Pilot Free Trade Zones (2015)
61. Lauren Gloudeman and Nargiza Salidjanova (2016) Policy Considerations for Negotiating a U.S.-China Bilateral Investment Treaty. https://www.uscc.gov/sites/default/files/Research/Staff%20Report_Policy%20Considerations%20for%20Negotiating%20a%20U.S.-China%20Bilateral%20Investment%20Treaty080116.pdf. Accessed 7 August 2025
62. Mark Magnier (2018) U.S.-China Investment Treaty Talks Cause Strain Ahead of Presidential Summit. Wall Street Journal. https://www.wsj.com/articles/u-s-china-investment-treaty-talks-cause-strain-ahead-of-presidential-summit-1442576345. Accessed 7 August 2025
63. The Decision of the Standing Committee of the National People's Congress on Amending Four Laws including the Law of the People's Republic of China on Wholly Foreign-Owned Enterprises (2016)
64. Interim Measures for the Recordation Administration of the Formation and Modification of Foreign-Funded Enterprises (2016)
65. Special Administrative Measures (Negative List) for the Access of Foreign Investment (2018)

66. Foreign Investment Law of the People's Republic of China (2019)
67. Seung Chong and Chin Leng Lim (2015) The Convergence of China's Foreign and Domestic Investment Regimes and China's Investment Treaty Commitments. Journal of International Arbitration, Volume 32, Issue 5: 461-492
68. The Measures for the Reporting of Foreign Investment Information (2019)
69. Measures for the Security Review of Foreign Investment (2020)
70. Jingjie Yang (2013) Reform 2.0 to be Unveiled. Global Times. https://www.globaltimes.cn/content/823892.shtml. Accessed 7 August 2025
71. Decision of the CCCPC on Some Major Issues Concerning Comprehensively Deepening the Reform (2013).
72. Axel Berger (2015) Hesitant Embrace: China's Recent Approach to International Investment Rule-Making. The Journal of World Investment & Trade, Volume 16, Issue 5-6: 843-868
73. China-Japan-Korea Trilateral Investment Agreement (2012)
74. China-EU Comprehensive Agreement on Investment (2020)
75. European Commission, EU-China agreement explained. https://policy.trade.ec.europa.eu/eu-trade-relationships-country-and-region/countries-and-regions/china/eu-china-agreement/agreement-explained_en. Accessed 7 August 2025
76. The Guiding Opinions of the CPC Central Committee and the State Council on Deepening the Reform of State-owned Enterprises (2015)

# Chapter 3
# Investment Protection: Substantive Standards

This chapter analyzes the substantive standards of investment protection in China's fourth-generation investment treaties. It begins by introducing the broader context of ongoing investment treaty reforms (Sect. 3.1). Next, it systematically traces the evolution of China's approach to substantive investment protection across the first three generations (Sect. 3.2) before focusing on the emerging fourth generation (Sect. 3.3). The analysis of the fourth generation focuses on five key substantive provisions: (1) definitions of investment and investor; (2) national treatment and MFN treatment; (3) fair and equitable treatment and full protection and security; (4) indirect expropriation; and (5) exception clauses.

## 3.1 Reforming the Investment Treaty Regime

The protection of foreign investment, at the beginning of the twentieth century, was mainly governed by customary international law [1]. However, this legal status became uncertain under the Russian and Mexican revolutions, during which the concept of private property was questioned, and different views were expressed as to compensation standards for expropriation [2]. As a response, in the 1938 US-Mexican correspondence, the US proposed that no government was "entitled to expropriate [foreign-owned] private property, for whatever purpose, without provision for prompt, adequate and effective payment"—known as the "Hull Formula" [2].

In 1948, the Havana Charter attempted to establish a multilateral investment agreement but finally failed due to different views among countries on "the interpretation of customary investment law and the content of international minimum standards of treatment for foreign investors" [1, 3]. The efforts subsequently turned to the bilateral level. In 1959, the first BIT was concluded between Germany and Pakistan, and

 
J. Chao, *The Emerging Fourth Generation of Chinese Investment Treaties*,
https://doi.org/10.1007/978-981-95-5052-4_3

subsequently, BITs became the primary legal instrument to provide protection for foreign investors [1, 4].

Undoubtedly, BITs initially focused on expropriation and compensation. For example, the 1959 Germany-Pakistan BIT, at Article 3(2), provided that "[n]ationals or companies of either Party *shall not be subjected to expropriation* of their investments in the territory of the other Party *except for public benefit against compensation*, which shall represent the equivalent of the investments affected. *Such compensation shall be actually realizable and freely transferable in the currency of the other Party without undue delay... The legality of any such expropriation and the amount of compensation shall be subject to review by due process of law*" [4].

In 1965, the ICSID was established, introducing a specialized mechanism for the settlement of investor-state disputes. Prior to this, investment disputes were predominantly resolved through inter-state adjudication [2]. The creation of ICSID, and the subsequent incorporation of ISDS provisions in BITs, marked a significant shift in investment dispute resolution. These developments enabled foreign investors to bring claims directly against host states through arbitration proceedings without the intervention of their home states [2]. This process was regarded as depoliticizing investment dispute resolution and enhancing protection for foreign investors [1, 2].

With the fall of the Berlin Wall in 1989 and the dissolution of the Soviet Union in 1991, the 1990s witnessed the dominance of neo-liberalism. The neo-liberalism, as Sornarajah argued, "advocated definite principles that stress trade without barriers, the flow of investments without hindrance, the protection of investment assets through secure recognition of private property, and dispute resolution mechanism to ensure compliance with standards of governance" [5]. As a result, BITs proliferated, with the number increasing from around 300 at the end of the 1980s to over 2,000 by the end of 2000 [1]. Many developing countries, especially those from Latin America, concluded a large number of BITs to compete for foreign investments. Furthermore, the first investment arbitration, *AAPL v. Sri Lanka*, was concluded in 1990 [1, 6].

However, with an increasing number of ISDS cases brought by investors, countries started to find that BITs would "bite" [7]. Specifically, most BITs concluded at that time contained broad and vague formulations and included few exceptions or safeguards [7]. According to UNCTAD, such broad and vague investment treaties can be regarded as "old-generation investment treaties" and most of them were concluded between 1959 and 2011 [8]. These features allowed foreign investors to challenge host states' core public policy, especially concerning environmental protection, financial stability, energy, and public health [7]. As a result, the regulatory space of countries was largely constrained by investment treaties. In addition, these features resulted in unanticipated and inconsistent arbitral interpretations of investment treaty provisions, which generated serious criticisms from countries and NGOs [7].

Today, there is a broadly shared view that the relationship between the protection of foreign investment and the right of states to regulate should be rebalanced. The balancing practice has been mainly achieved through two ways: (1) the clarification of substantive protection provisions reflecting on the existing arbitral practice, which will be discussed in this Chapter, and (2) the reform of the ISDS mechanism, which will be discussed in next Chapter. According to UNCTAD, the balanced investment treaties, most of which were concluded after 2012, mark a new era of investment treaty making and should be regarded as "new-generation investment treaties" [8].

## 3.2 Substantive Protection Under the First Three Generations of Chinese Investment Treaties

### *3.2.1 China's Previous Treaty Commitments*

As outlined in Chap. 1, Chinese investment treaties concluded from 1982 to 2007 fall into three generations: (1) 1982–1989, (2) 1990–1997, and (3) 1998–2007. Under these three generations, China's approach to investment protection gradually shifted from conservative to liberal. The substantive protection standards of each generation are analyzed below.

#### 3.2.1.1 China's First-Generation Investment Treaties

The first generation of Chinese investment treaties started with the 1982 China-Sweden BIT. At the time, China had just opened its doors to the world, and the BIT program was launched to provide foreign investors with legal assurance and confidence to attract their investment [9]. Consequently, many of China's first-generation investment treaties were concluded with Western European countries, including Germany, France, Finland, the United Kingdom, and so forth [9]. Regarding substantive investment protection standards, Chinese Model BIT Version I serves as a representative example.

One of the most notable features of Version I was that no national treatment was granted to foreign investors [10]. The absence of national treatment provisions reflected China's restrictive regulatory regime for foreign investment, as discussed in Chap. 2. In addition, Version I provided MFN treatment only in a limited way—applying solely to "fair and equitable treatment and protection" provision [10]. The "fair and equitable treatment and protection" provision stipulated that "[i]nvestments and activities associated with investments of investors of either Contracting Party shall be accorded *fair and equitable treatment and shall enjoy protection* in the territory of the other Contracting party" [10]. As will be demonstrated below, the term "protection" was subsequently revised to "constant protection and security" in the second and third generations [11, 12]. Gallager and Shan argued that these formulations represented variations of the "full protection and security" standard and the inclusion of qualifications like "full" and "constant" indicated "stronger commitment or wider coverage" [9]. For example, the tribunal in *Azurix v Argentina* stated that when the "protection and security" was qualified by "full", the content of this obligation extended beyond physical protection and may overlap with the FET standard [9, 13].

Furthermore, Version I only provided that the compensation for expropriation would be "equivalent to the value of the expropriated investments at the time when expropriation is proclaimed, be convertible and freely transferable" [10]. There was no mention of "market value", suggesting that China held some skeptics about the "Hull Formula"—the "prompt, adequate and effective" compensation. However, Version I defined "investment" broadly as "every kind of asset invested by investors of one Contracting Party in accordance with the laws and regulations of the other Contracting Party", followed by a non-exclusive list of assets as examples [10]. Version I also broadly defined "investor" as "natural persons who have nationality" or "economic entities established in accordance with the laws"[10]. These broad definitions were similarly incorporated in the Version II and Version III of Chinese Model BIT [11, 12]. As will be demonstrated below, in China's investment arbitration cases, a key issue concerned the definition of investor—specifically whether Chinese SOEs were entitled to protection under Chinese investment treaties.

Overall, the substantive investment protection provided under China's first-generation investment treaties was relatively limited, especially regarding national treatment. This limitation reflected China's conservative approach to investment protection at the time.

#### 3.2.1.2 China's Second-Generation Investment Treaties

China's second-generation investment treaties spanned the period from 1990 to 1997. As noted, the 1990s was the golden age of BITs, as many developing countries concluded investment treaties to compete for foreign investments. China actively participated in this BIT proliferation, with approximately half of its existing investment treaties being concluded during this period [9]. Regarding substantive protection standards, Version II of Chinese Model BIT introduced two significant modifications.

First, Version II began to incorporate national treatment provisions, but such treatments were granted "to the extent possible" and "in accordance with the stipulations of its laws and regulations" [11]. This best-effort clause reflected China's continued adherence to a restrictive foreign investment regulatory framework.

Second, Version II revised the wording of the FET provision as follows:

> "Investment made by investors of each contracting party shall at all times be *accorded fair and equitable treatment and shall enjoy constant protection and security* in the territory of the other contracting party. Neither contracting party, shall without prejudice to its laws and regulations, *in any way impair by unreasonable or discriminatory measures* the management, maintenance, use, enjoyment or disposal of investments in its territory of investors of the other contracting party. Each contracting party shall observe any obligations it may have entered into with regard to investments of investors of the other contracting party." [11]

Gallager and Shan argued that the prohibition of unreasonable or discriminatory measures should complement, rather than diminish, the FET obligation [9]. As will be analyzed below, arbitral jurisprudence has developed several elements for the

FET obligation, one of which specifically addresses arbitrary and discriminatory treatment.

Overall, under the second generation, Chinese investment treaties increased substantive protection standards but still maintained a conservative approach to investment protection.

#### 3.2.1.3 China's Third-Generation Investment Treaties

From 1998 to 2007, Chinese investment treaties transitioned into their third generation, marking a complete shift from a conservative to a liberal approach. During this period, China's third-generation investment treaties were regarded as conforming to "what can be considered as standard treaty practice in approximately 2500 BITs worldwide" [14].

Regarding substantive protection standards, the most significant development was the inclusion of qualified national treatment provisions. As discussed in Chap. 2, these provisions took two forms: the first type granted national treatment subject to domestic laws and regulations, while the second type subjected national treatment to a grandfather clause for existing non-conforming measures [12, 15]. More significantly, under the second type, China committed to refraining from introducing new non-conforming measures [15].

Overall, this liberal approach ensured that China's third-generation investment treaties provided comprehensive protection for foreign investors.

### *3.2.2 Arbitral Tribunals' Treaty Interpretations*

As discussed in Chap. 1, so far there have been 28 cases initiated under Chinese investment treaties. A closer examination of these cases shows that most stalled at the jurisdiction stage, especially concerning the interpretation of restrictive ISDS provisions. As noted, regarding substantive protection standards, a key issue was whether Chinese SOEs were entitled to protection under Chinese investment treaties. This issue was addressed in detail in *Beijing Urban Construction v. Yemen.*

The *Beijing Urban Construction v. Yemen* case involved the construction of an airport terminal in Yemen. In its Decision on Jurisdiction, the tribunal adopted the "Broches test" to determine whether Beijing Urban Construction, as a Chinese SOE, could be protected under the 1998 China-Yemen BIT [16]. The Broches test provided that:

> "… for purposes of the Convention a mixed economy company or government- owned corporation *should not be disqualified as a "national of another Contracting State" unless it is acting as an agent for the government or is discharging an essentially governmental function.*" [16]

It was further emphasized that during the determination, "the focus must be on the nature of these activities and not their purpose"[16].

Based on these standards, the tribunal examined the following three questions:

(1) Whether Beijing Urban Construction acted as an agent for the Chinese government in the project: on this point, Yemen submitted a variety of Chinese government documents to show that Chinese SOEs were required to promote national interests. However, the tribunal stated that "the issue is not the corporate framework of the State-owned enterprise, but whether it functions as an agent of the State in the *facts -specific context*" [16]. In this case, these documents could not demonstrate that Beijing Urban Construction acted as an agent for the Chinese government in building the airport terminal [16].

(2) Whether Beijing Urban Construction discharged "an essentially governmental function" in the construction work: the tribunal again ruled that, based on the evidence, the role of Beijing Urban Construction was merely commercial and did not involve governmental functions [16].

(3) Whether Beijing Urban Construction was required to register its investment in Yemen: the tribunal confirmed that the BIT did not impose such a requirement [16].

Ultimately, the tribunal dismissed Yemen's objections regarding the SOE's status. Nevertheless, interpretation risks remain due to the discretion of arbitral tribunals. Therefore, it is advisable for China's fourth-generation investment treaties to explicitly include SOEs in the definition of investor.

## 3.3 Balancing Practice Under the Fourth Generation of Chinese Investment Treaties

As stated above, within the context of neo-liberal dominance, China's third- generation investment treaties were highly valued, marking a significant shift from a conservative to a liberal approach. However, after experiencing investment arbitration cases, many countries began reformulating their investment treaties in the early 2000s to preserve greater regulatory space for host states. Although China did not encounter its first investment arbitration case until 2007, Chinese scholars had already initiated a critical examination of the liberal approach prior to that.

Chinese scholars' criticisms over this liberal approach were marked by a book titled *New Development in International Investment Law and New Practice of China's Bilateral Investment Treaties* published in 2007 (in Chinese) [17]. As for the future development of Chinese investment treaties, Chen suggested that China should provide different reciprocity treatments to two types of countries—North and South [18]. Cai held that China would no longer need to conclude BITs with developed countries, as there was no clear correlation between concluding BITs and attracting foreign investment [19]. When negotiating BITs with developing countries, China, in Cai's view, should adopt a development-oriented model to align with the "specific stage of national development" [19].

As a response, Gallagher and Shan argued in their 2009 monograph *Chinese Investment Treaties: Policies and Practice* that China should update its Model BIT [9]. They maintained that the new Model BIT should adopt a single text, rather than "dual or multiple texts for different treaty partners", as the dual-text approach was inconsistent with general treaty practice and violated the principle of non-discrimination [9]. Furthermore, they emphasized that the new Model BIT should strike a balance between the rights and obligations of host states and foreign investors, as China had emerged as a major capital exporter and increasingly aligned itself with the positions of developed capital-exporting counties [9].

Beyond this scholarly debate, recent Chinese investment treaties has demonstrated that China did not revert to its previous conservative BIT approach. Instead, since 2008, Chinese investment treaties have gradually shifted toward balancing the protection of foreign investment and the right of states to regulate. China's balancing practice has drawn lessons from US experience, especially the 2004 US Model BIT [20]. Some scholars have termed this process as the "Americanization" or "NAFTA-zation" [21, 22]. However, China did not adopt the US balancing approach all at once. Rather, the recalibration of Chinese investment treaties has been incremental, primarily achieved through modifications to five key substantive provisions. The specifics of China's balancing practice are examined in detail below.

## 3.3.1 Definitions of Investment and Investor

### 3.3.1.1 Definition of Investment

According to UNCTAD, old-generation investment treaties defined "investment" very broadly, basically covering all kinds of assets [23]. This is also the case for the first three generations of Chinese investment treaties. For example, Chinese Model BIT Version III defined investment as "every kind of asset invested by investors of one Contracting Party in accordance with the laws and regulations of the other Contracting Party" [12]. Following this broad definition, a non-exclusive list of examples was also included.

In arbitral practice, the Salini test has been developed to help interpret such an open-ended definition of investment. It provides that an investment should satisfy four requirements, including "[i] contributions, [ii] a certain duration of performance of the contract and [iii] a participation in the risks of the transaction ...[iv] the contribution to the economic development of the host state of the investment" [24]. The Salini test has been recognized by many tribunals due to its clarity. However, some tribunals have not adhered to these standards, as investment arbitration does not adopt the doctrine of precedent [23]. This creates uncertainty regarding what types of investments can be covered by investment treaties and enjoy investment treaty protection.

Considering this, many countries have begun to incorporate the Salini test into their investment treaties to further clarify the definition of investment [23]. For example, the 2016 CETA requires that investment should include "a certain duration and other characteristics such as the commitment of capital or other resources, the expectation of gain or profit, or the assumption of risk" [25]. Similarly, the 2018 CPTPP requires that investments should have the characteristics of "the commitment of capital or other resources, the expectation of gain or profit, or the assumption of risk" [26].

The post-2008 Chinese investment treaties also require that investment should fulfill some specific characteristics. For example, the 2012 China-Japan-Korea TIT requires "the commitment of capital or other resources, the expectation gain or profit, or the assumption of risk" [27]; the 2015 China-Australia FTA requires "the commitment of capital or other resources, the expectation of gain or profit, or the assumption of risk" [28]; and the 2020 RCEP requires "the commitment of capital or other resources, the expectation of gains or profits, or the assumption of risk" [29]. These provisions are nearly identical, reflecting a clear alignment with the CPTPP treaty practice.

According to UNCTAD, in addition to specifying investment characteristics, new-generation investment treaties often exclude certain types of assets from the definition of investment to address the issues encountered in arbitral practice [23]. Furthermore, the most commonly excluded three items include: (1) "debt issued by a party or loans granted to a party" as in the case of the 2018 CPTPP; (2) "claims to money arising solely from commercial contracts for the sale of goods and services" as in the cases of the 2016 CETA, 2018 CPTPP, and 2018 USMCA; and (3) "any order or judgment entered in a judicial or administrative action" as in the case of the 2018 USMCA [23].

In the post-2008 Chinese investment treaties, the 2012 China-Canada BIT explicitly excludes "claims to money", whereas the 2012 China-Japan-Korea TIT and the 2015 China-Australia FTA contain no such exclusions [27, 28, 30]. This inconsistency in China's treaty practice is likely because these treaties were concluded during the early phase of fourth generation. However, the 2020 RCEP marks a shift by excluding all three of the most commonly excluded items, reflecting contemporary trends in investment treaty making [29].

Overall, China's fourth-generation investment treaties have primarily adopted two methods to refine the broad definition of investment: (1) requiring investments to fulfill certain characteristics, thereby incorporating and reinforcing the Salini test; and (2) explicitly excluding certain types of assets from investment definition, thereby addressing controversies on the scope of covered investments in arbitral practice.

#### 3.3.1.2 Definition of Investor

Regarding the definition of investor, according to UNCTAD, the clarification practice primarily addresses two aspects: First, for a natural person, recent investment treaties explicitly address dual nationality, as in the cases of the 2016 CETA and 2018

USMCA [23, 25, 31]. Since China does not recognize dual nationality, the applicability of these provisions depends on the legal framework of the other contracting party [32].

Second, for a legal entity, additional requirements are introduced, such as having a seat and/or engaging in substantial business activities in host states [23]. This is seen in treaties like the 2016 CETA and 2018 CPTPP [25, 26]. For China, Chinese Model BIT Version III required that legal entities should be "incorporated or constituted under the laws and regulations of either Contracting Party and have their seats in that Contracting Party" [12]. Under the fourth generation, the 2015 China-Australia FTA and the 2020 RCEP introduced the substantial business activities requirement [28, 29]. These requirements aim to "exclude 'shell' companies from the scope of the investment treaty" [20].

Overall, China's fourth-generation investment treaties have significantly clarified the definition of investor. However, as noted, China's investment arbitration practice reveals a recurring issue regarding whether Chinese SOEs qualify as protected investors under these treaties. This jurisdictional issue may be frequently raised by respondent states when claims are brought by Chinese SOEs. Although the arbitral tribunal in *Beijing Urban Construction v. Yemen* applied the Broches test and ruled in favor of Chinese SOEs, it is advisable for China's fourth-generation investment treaties to explicitly address this issue. Such clarification holds particular significance for China, given approximately half of China's OFDI projects are undertaken by Chinese SOEs [33, 34].

In fact, some recent Chinese investment treaties have begun to address this issue. For example, the 2012 China-Canada BIT defines "enterprises" as:

> "[A]ny entity constituted or organized in accordance with the laws of a Contracting Party, *such as public institutions, corporations, foundations, agencies, cooperatives, trust, societies, associations and similar entities* and private companies, firms, partnerships, establishments, joint ventures and organizations, whether or not for profit, and irrespective of whether their liabilities are limited or otherwise…" [30]

Furthermore, the 2012 China-Japan-Korea TIT, 2015 China-Korea FTA, 2015 China-Australia FTA and 2020 RCEP defines "enterprises" or "judicial person" as:

> "[A]ny legal person or any other entity constituted or organized under the applicable laws and regulations of that Contracting Party, *whether or not for profit, and whether private-or government-owned or controlled*, and includes a company, corporation, trust, partnership, sole proprietorship, joint venture, association or organization…" [27–29, 35]

These two approaches clearly establish that SOEs are entitled to the same treaty protection as private companies. Comparatively, the second approach provides more concise and explicit wording. In fact, this approach originates from the 2004 US Model BIT, which subsequently influenced the 2012 US Model BIT, 2016 CETA, 2018 CPTPP, and 2018 USMCA. This demonstrates an emerging international consensus regarding SOEs as qualified investors. Nevertheless, to mitigate potential arbitration risks, China's fourth-generation investment treaties should adopt explicit provisions mirroring the second approach.

### *3.3.2 National Treatment and Most-Favored-Nation Treatment*

#### 3.3.2.1 National Treatment

Regarding national treatment, it is generally understood that foreign investors should be granted the same treatment as domestic investors in like circumstances. However, under the broad and vague provisions in old-generation investment treaties, some arbitral tribunals ruled in favor of national treatment even when circumstances were not deemed "like" [23]. Consequently, new-generation investment treaties have explicitly specified that national treatment applies only in "like circumstances" and some of these treaties have further listed specific factors for determining what constitutes "like circumstances" [23].

For example, the 2018 CPTPP at Article 9.4 and its footnote provides:

> "Each Party shall accord to investors of another Party treatment no less favourable than that it accords, *in like circumstances,* to its own investors with respect to the establishment, acquisition, expansion, management, conduct, operation, and sale or other disposition of investments in its territory.
>
> For greater certainty, whether treatment is accorded in "like circumstances" under Article 9.4 (National Treatment) or Article 9.5 (Most-Favoured-Nation Treatment) *depends on the totality of the circumstances, including whether the relevant treatment distinguishes between investors or investments on the basis of legitimate public welfare objectives.*" [26]

Most post-2008 Chinese investment treaties have explicitly provided that national treatment should be granted "in like circumstances" but have not gone further listing specific considerations. This is seen in the 2012 China-Canada BIT, 2012 China-Japan-Korea TIT, 2015 China-Korea FTA, and 2015 China-Australia FTA [27, 28, 30, 35]. However, the 2020 RCEP marks a shift by both referring to "like circumstances" and clarifying specific considerations for determination [29]. Therefore, the RCEP practice could serve as a model for China's future fourth-generation investment treaties.

#### 3.3.2.2 Most-Favored-Nation Treatment

As for the MFN treatment—which requires treating foreign investors no less favorably than investors from other countries—the "like circumstances" qualification similarly applies [23]. Another significant issue concerns whether investors may rely on MFN clauses to invoke more-friendly ISDS provisions [23]. This is also especially relevant to China, given that its first and second-generation investment treaties contained restrictive ISDS provisions permitting only "disputes concerning the amount of compensation for expropriation" to be submitted to international arbitration, while its third-generation investment treaties adopted comprehensive ISDS provisions covering "all kinds of disputes" [10–12].

In China's investment arbitration cases, such MFN claims have consistently been dismissed, as evidenced in *Tza Yap Shum v. Peru* and *Sanum v. Laos*. However, most post-2008 Chinese investment treaties have expressly addressed this matter [36, 37]. For example, the 2020 RCEP provides that "[f]or greater certainty, the treatment referred to in paragraphs 1 and 2 does *not encompass any international dispute resolution procedures or mechanisms under other existing or future international agreements*" [29]. Similar provisions appear in the 2012 China-Canada BIT, 2012 China-Japan-Korea TIT, 2015 China-Korea FTA, and 2015 China-Australia FTA [27, 28, 30, 35].

### *3.3.3 Fair and Equitable Treatment and Full Protection and Security*

The FET and FPS standards are among the most controversial provisions in investment treaties. The old-generation investment treaties simply stated that investors should be granted FET and FPS. This is also the case for the first three generations of Chinese investment treaties [10–12]. However, arbitral practice has interpreted the FET standard as encompassing a variety of elements, including arbitrary and discriminatory treatment, violation of due process, lack of transparency, bad faith, violation of investors' legitimate expectations and so forth [2]. Similarly, the FPS standard has been expansively interpreted to include "economic, legal and other protection and security" [23]. Consequently, it is necessary to clarify the scope of FET and FPS standards.

Generally, there are two approaches in the investment treaty practice to clarify the scope of FET and FPS standards. The first one is a non-exhaustive list approach. This approach was first adopted in the 2004 US Model BIT as follows:

> "1. Each Party shall accord to covered investments treatment *in accordance with customary international law, including fair and equitable treatment and full protection and security.*
>
> 2. For greater certainty, paragraph 1 prescribes the customary international law minimum standard of treatment of aliens as the minimum standard of treatment to be afforded to covered investments. The concepts of "fair and equitable treatment" and "full protection and security" *do not require treatment in addition to or beyond that which is required by that standard, and do not create additional substantive rights.* The obligation in paragraph 1 to provide:
>
> (a) "fair and equitable treatment" *includes the obligation not to deny justice in criminal, civil, or administrative adjudicatory proceedings in accordance with the principle of due process embodied in the principal legal systems of the world*; and
> (b) "full protection and security" requires each Party to *provide the level of police protection* required under customary international law.
>
> 3. A determination that *there has been a breach of another provision* of this Treaty, or of a separate international agreement, *does not establish that there has been a breach of this Article.*" [38]

As seen above, the FET and FPS standards were initially linked to customary international law, before several clarifications were provided, including:

(1) Customary international law was set as a ceiling to the FET and FPS standards. This clarification stemmed from the 2001 NAFTA Free Trade Commission (FTC) Interpretation Note, as the FET and FPS provisions in the NAFTA—providing "[e]ach Party shall accord to …treatment in accordance with international law, including fair and equitable treatment and full protection and security"—generated much controversy as to the relationship between (customary) international law and the FET and FPS standards [39, 40].
(2) Some examples were provided for the scope of FET and FPS standards. For example, the FET standard included "the obligation not to deny justice in criminal, civil, or administrative adjudicatory proceedings" [38]. These examples reflected arbitral practice, but it should be noted that this did not constitute an exclusive list [39].
(3) It was further stated that a violation of other provisions did not establish a violation of the FET and FPS obligations. This statement also stemmed from the 2001 NAFTA FTC Interpretation Note to respond to awards like *S.D. Myers v. Canada* [39, 41].

It is noteworthy that the 2004 US Model BIT at its Annex also defined customary international law as follows:

> "The Parties confirm their shared understanding that 'customary international law' generally and as specifically referenced in Article 5 [Minimum Standard of Treatment] and Annex B [Expropriation] *results from a general and consistent practice of States that they follow from a sense of legal obligation.* With regard to Article 5 [Minimum Standard of Treatment], the customary international law minimum standard of treatment of aliens refers to all customary international law principles that protect the economic rights and interests of aliens." [38]

Vandevelde argued that this definition originated from the Sect. 102 of the Third Restatement of the US Foreign Relations Law, aiming to direct arbitral tribunals to resort to state practice in interpretating customary international law [39, 42]. The first approach has subsequently been followed by the 2012 US Model BIT, 2018 CPTPP, and 2018 USMCA [26, 31, 43].

The post-2008 Chinese investment treaties did not adopt all these clarifications simultaneously. Instead, these treaties have adopted these clarifications inconsistently. For example, the first clarification has raised several issues: (1) with or without reference: some recent Chinese investment treaties, such as the 2009 China-ASEAN investment agreement, contain no reference to the FET and FPS standards [44]; (2) what reference: customary international law is referred both directly and indirectly, as evidenced in the 2009 China-Peru FTA and the 2012 China-Canada BIT [30, 45].In contrast, the 2008 China-New Zealand FTA and the 2012 China-Japan-Korea TIT refer to "international law" or "generally accepted rules of international law" [27, 46]; (3) what relationship between the reference and the FET and FPS standards: no uniform clarification exists on this point. As Shan and Chen explain, such inconsistent BIT practice suggests that China has been "qualifying the standard to make sure that it is not misused" [33].

Furthermore, many recent Chinese investment treaties have incorporated the second and third clarifications. For example, the 2009 China-ASEAN investment agreement provides that the FET refers to "the obligation of each Party not to deny justice in any legal or administrative proceedings" [44]. It further provides that the FPS standard requires each Party to "take such measures as may be reasonably necessary to ensure the protection and security of the investment of investors of another Party" [44]. It also clarifies that a breach of another treaty provision could not establish a breach of the FET and FPS provisions [44].

Despite inconsistencies, recent Chinese investment treaties have increasingly aligned their formulations of the FET and FPS standards with the 2004 US Model BIT. Notably, the minimum standard of treatment provision in the 2015 China-Korea FTA closely mirrors those in the 2004 and 2012 US Model BIT [35, 38, 43]. This FTA's annex on customary international law is virtually identical to those in the 2004 and 2012 US Model BIT [35, 38, 43]. This development is particularly significant given China's longstanding skepticism and hesitation toward accepting customary international law.

One may wonder whether these FET and FPS clarifications would yield any practical difference. In arbitral practice, several tribunals have similar reservations. For example, the *Azurix v. Argentina* tribunal concluded that setting customary international law as a ceiling to the FET and FPS standards concerned "a question about the substantive content of FET", and "whichever side of the argument one takes, the answer to the question may in substance be the same" [13]. The *Rumeli v Kazakhstan* tribunal further argued that the scope of FET and FPS standards was ultimately determined by tribunals and tribunals would "have to decide whether in all the circumstances the conduct in issue is fair and equitable or unfair and inequitable" [47].

As previously discussed, arbitral jurisprudence has developed several elements constituting the content of the FET and FPS standards. Given that tribunals' persistent interpretive discretion, several countries, notably the EU and India, have developed the second approach—the exhaustive/closed-list approach—to further clarify the scope of FET and FPS standards.

Specifically, the 2016 CETA at Art 8.10 provides that:

> "1. Each Party shall accord in its territory to covered investments of the other Party and to investors with respect to their covered investments *fair and equitable treatment and full protection and security in accordance with paragraphs 2 through 7.*
>
> 2. A Party breaches the obligation of fair and equitable treatment referenced in paragraph 1 *if a measure or series of measures constitutes*:
>
> (a) denial of justice in criminal, civil or administrative proceedings;
> (b) fundamental breach of due process, including a fundamental breach of transparency, in judicial and administrative proceedings;
> (c) manifest arbitrariness;
> (d) targeted discrimination on manifestly wrongful grounds, such as gender, race or religious belief;
> (e) abusive treatment of investors, such as coercion, duress and harassment; or
> (f) a breach of any further elements of the fair and equitable treatment obligation adopted by the Parties in accordance with paragraph 3 of this Article.

> 3. The Parties shall *regularly, or upon request of a Party, review the content of the obligation to provide fair and equitable treatment*. The *Committee on Services and Investment*, established under Article 26.2.1(b) (Specialised committees), *may develop recommendations in this regard and submit them to the CETA Joint Committee for decision.*
>
> 4. When applying the above fair and equitable treatment obligation, a Tribunal *may take into account whether a Party made a specific representation to an investor to induce a covered investment, that created a legitimate expectation, and upon which the investor relied in deciding to make or maintain the covered investment, but that the Party subsequently frustrated.*
>
> 5. For greater certainty, "full protection and security" *refers to the Party's obligations relating to the physical security* of investors and covered investments.
>
> 6. For greater certainty, *a breach of another provision* of this Agreement, or of a separate international agreement *does not establish a breach of this Article.*
>
> 7. For greater certainty, the fact that a measure breaches domestic law does not, in and of itself, establish a breach of this Article. In order to ascertain whether the measure breaches this Article, a Tribunal must consider whether a Party has acted inconsistently with the obligations in paragraph 1." [25]

As seen above, compared with the first approach, the second approach lists all elements that tribunals may consider in determining FET and FPS violations. Under this framework: (1) tribunals are strictly confined to the list of elements; (2) contracting states need to regularly review these elements; (3) the Committee on Services and Investment may formulate and submit recommendations to the CETA Joint Committee for decision. The EU maintains that this provision "defines precisely the content of the standard without leaving unwelcome discretion to arbitrators" [48].

However, some commentators have expressed skepticism regarding the EU's exhaustive/closed-list approach. For example, Shan and Chen argued that the EU's approach might not be very different from the US approach, as the terms like "fundamental" and "manifest" could leave room for discretionary interpretations [33]. Furthermore, Bernasconi-Osterwalder pointed out that "the language used in the CETA list reflects, in large part, the language of the *Waste Management II* decision" [49]. Therefore, China may need to seriously consider the EU's approach.

It is also worth noting that the 2016 CETA specifically addresses the issue of investors' legitimate expectations. The violation of legitimate expectations has been the most controversial FET element. In response, the 2016 CETA does not incorporate this element in the scope of FET standard. Instead, it provides that "legitimate expectations may only be treated as a relevant consideration" when assessing these listed FET elements [50]. Similarly, the 2018 CPTPP clarifies that "[f]or greater certainty, *the mere fact that a Party takes or fails to take an action that may be inconsistent with an investor's expectations does not constitute a breach of this Article*, even if there is loss or damage to the covered investment as a result" [26]. However, recent Chinese investment treaties, including the 2020 RCEP, do not specifically address this issue [29].

Overall, the post-2008 Chinese investment treaties have adopted the first approach to clarify the scope of FET and FPS standards. However, given the ongoing debate over the expansive interpretation of the FET and FPS standards and the progress of China-EU negotiations on substantive investment protection, it remains to be seen how China's future fourth-generation investment treaties will clarify the FET and FPS standards. It is suggested that China consider whether the EU's exhaustive/closed-list approach could effectively achieve its objective of further limiting expansive interpretations. Additionally, China should further address the issue of investors' legitimate expectations to align with contemporary trends in investment treaty practice.

### 3.3.4 Indirect Expropriation

Today, it is indirect expropriation that generates the most controversy and criticism. The 2004 US Model BIT introduced an expropriation annex defining and clarifying indirect expropriation, which has significantly influenced many countries' treaty practice (including the EU, Canada, Japan, and China) [38]. For example, in the Annex B of the 2012 China-Canada BIT, indirect expropriation is firstly defined as "a measure or series of measures of a Contracting Party that has an effect equivalent to direct expropriation without formal transfer of title or outright seizure" [30].

Annex B further clarifies that the determination of whether a measure or series of measures constitutes an indirect expropriation should be based on the fact and examined on a case-by-case basis [30]. Three factors are also listed for the tribunals' consideration:

> "(i) *the economic impact of the measure or series of measures*, although the sole fact that a measure or series of measures of a Contracting Party has an adverse effect on the economic value of an investment does not establish that an indirect expropriation has occurred;
>
> (ii) *the extent to* which the measure or series of measures *interferes with distinct, reasonable, investment-backed expectations*; and
>
> (iii) the *character of the measure or series of measures*." [30]

Annex B also introduces an expropriation exception—"except in rare circumstances", nondiscriminatory regulatory measures adopted to protect legitimate public policies do not constitute indirect expropriation [30]. This exception was first adopted in the 2004 US Model BIT, stemming from the US arguments in the *Methanex v. US* case for preserving greater regulatory space of the host state [39, 51].

These clarifications also appear in the 2012 China-Japan-Korea TIT, 2015 China-Korea FTA, 2015 China-Australia FTA, and 2020 RCEP [27–29, 35]. Overall, China's fourth-generation investment treaties have established a comprehensive approach to clarify indirect expropriation.

### 3.3.5 Exception Clauses

None of the three versions of Chinses Model BITs incorporated exception clauses [10–12]. However, in its fourth-generation investment treaties, China has sought to preserve greater regulatory space for host states by introducing various exception clauses. A prime example is the 2012 China-Canada BIT, which establishes a comprehensive set of exception clauses with seven specific policy areas carved out [30].

First, it carves out cultural industries, providing that "nothing in this agreement shall apply to measures in respect of cultural industries" [30]. The term "cultural industries" primarily encompasses activities related to the publication, production, distribution, sale or exhibition of books, magazines, film, audio, video recordings and so forth [30].

Second, it adopts an exception provision for environmental protection. Specifically, it provides that nothing shall prevent a Contracting Party from adopting or maintaining environmental measures that are "(a) necessary to ensure compliance with laws and regulations that are not inconsistent with the provisions of this Agreement"; "(b) necessary to protect human, animal, or plant life or health"; or "(c) relating to the conservation of living or non-living exhaustible natural resources if such measures are made effective in conjunction with restriction on domestic production or consumption" [30].

The third and fourth exceptions provide that nothing shall prevent a Contracting Party from adopting or maintaining reasonable measures for prudential reasons and for monetary or related credit policies or exchange rate policies [30]. The fifth one is a self-judging essential security exception, providing that nothing shall prevent a Contracting Party from "taking any *actions that it considers necessary* for the protection of its essential security interests" [30]. The sixth and seventh exceptions concern information security and the WTO agreement [30].

Overall, the comprehensive exception clauses in the 2012 China-Canada BIT serve as a good model for China's fourth generation investment treaties.

## 3.4 Conclusion

Over the past decade of treaty practice, China's fourth-generation investment treaties have established a balanced approach to investment protection by: (1) clarifying key treaty provisions—including definitions of investment and investor, national treatment and MFN treatment, FET and FPS standards, and indirect expropriation—to prevent expansive interpretations by arbitral tribunals; and (2) incorporating exception clauses to preserve greater regulatory space for host states. To further strengthen this balanced approach, China's fourth-generation treaties should address two critical issues: (1) the explicit inclusion of SOEs under the definition of investor; and (2) the treatment of investors' legitimate expectations under the FET standard. More significantly, China should maintain its refined balancing approach consistently in its future fourth-generation treaties, thereby effectively achieving the balance between investment protection and the right of states to regulate.

## References


1. UNCTAD (2015) World Investment Report 2015: Reforming International Investment Governance. Switzerland
2. Chin Leng Lim, Jean Ho and Martins Paparinskis (2018) International Investment Law and Arbitration: Commentary, Awards and other Materials, 1st edn. Cambridge
3. Havana Charter (1948)
4. Germany-Pakistan BIT (1959)
5. M. Sornarajah (2015) Resistance and Change in the International Law on Foreign Investment. Cambridge
6. Asian Agricultural Products Ltd. v. Republic of Sri Lanka, ICSID Case No. ARB/87/3
7. UNCTAD (2017) World Investment Report 2017: Investment and The Digital Economy. Switzerland
8. UNCTAD (2012) World Investment Report 2012: Towards A New Generation of Investment Policies. Switzerland
9. Norah Gallagher and Wenhua Shan (2009) Chinese Investment Treaties: Policies and Practice. Oxford
10. Chinese Model BIT Version I (1984)
11. Chinese Model BIT Version II (1989)
12. Chinese Model BIT Version III (1997)
13. Azurix Corp. v. The Argentine Republic, ICSID Case No. ARB/01/12
14. Stephen W. Schill (2007) Tearing Down the Great Wall: The New Generation Investment Treaties of the People's Republic of China. Cardozo Journal of International and Comparative Law, Volume 15, Issue 1: 73-115
15. China-Germany BIT (2003)
16. Beijing Urban Construction Group Co. Ltd. v. Republic of Yemen, ICSID Case No. ARB/14/30
17. An Chen and Congyan Cai (eds) (2007) New Development in International Investment Law and New Practice of China's Bilateral Investment Treaties (in Chinese: Guo ji tou zi fa de xin fa zhan yu Zhong guo Shuang bian tou zi tiao yue de xin shi jian). Fudan, Shanghai
18. An Chen (2007) Distinguishing Two Types of Countries and Properly Granting Differential Reciprocity Treatment-Re-Comments on the Four Safeguards in Sino-Foreign BITs Not to Be Hastily and Completely Dismantled. Journal of World Investment & Trade, Volume 8, Issue 6: 771-795
19. Congyan Cai (2007) Change of the Structure of International Investment and the Development of Developing Countries' BIT Practice. Journal of World Investment & Trade, Volume 8, Issue 6: 829-847
20. Elodie Dulac (2010) The Emerging Third Generation of Chinese Investment Treaties. Transnational Dispute Settlement 4
21. Congyan Cai (2009) China-US Negotiations and the Future of Investment Treaty Regime: A Grand Bilateral Bargain with Multilateral Implications. Journal of International Economic Law, Volume 12, Issue 2: 457-506
22. Axel Berger (2015) Hesitant Embrace: China's Recent Approach to International Investment Rule-Making. Journal of World Investment & Trade, Volume 16, Issue 5-6: 843-868
23. UNCTAD (2020) International Investment Agreements Reform Accelerator. Switzerland
24. Salini Costruttori S.p.A. and Italstrade S.p.A. v. Kingdom of Morocco [I], ICSID Case No. ARB/00/4
25. EU-Canada Comprehensive Economic and Trade Agreement (2016)
26. Comprehensive and Progressive Agreement for Trans-Pacific Partnership (2018)
27. China-Japan-Korea Trilateral Investment Agreement (2012)
28. China-Australia FTA (2015)
29. Regional Comprehensive Economic Partnership (2020)
30. China-Canada BIT (2012)

31. United States-Mexico-Canada Agreement (2018)
32. Nationality Law of the People's Republic of China (1980)
33. Wenhua Shan and Hongrui Chen (2016) China-US BIT Negotiation and the Emerging Chinese BIT 4.0. In: C. L. Lim (ed), Alternative Visions of the International Law on Foreign Investment: Essays in Honour of Muthucumaraswamy Sornarajah. Cambridge, p 223–254
34. Karl P. Sauvant and Michael D. Nolan (2015) China's Outward Foreign Direct Investment and International Investment Law. Journal of International Economic Law, Volume 18, Issue 4: 893–934
35. China-Korea FTA (2015)
36. Señor Tza Yap Shum v. The Republic of Peru, ICSID Case No. ARB/07/6
37. Sanum Investments v. Lao People's Democratic Republic (PCA Case No. 2013–13)
38. United States Model BIT (2004)
39. Kenneth. J. Vandevelde (2009) A Comparison of the 2004 and 1994 U.S. Model BITs: Rebalancing Investor and Host Country Interests. In: Karl. P. Sauvant (ed), Yearbook on International Investment Law & Policy 2008–2009. Oxford, p 283–316
40. North American Free Trade Agreement (1994)
41. S.D. Myers, Inc. v. Government of Canada, UNCITRAL
42. Restatement (Third) of US Foreign Relations Law (1987)
43. United States Model BIT (2012)
44. China-ASEAN investment agreement (2009)
45. China-Peru FTA (2009)
46. China-New Zealand FTA (2008)
47. Rumeli Telekom A.S. and Telsim Mobil Telekomunikasyon Hizmetleri A.S. v. Republic of Kazakhstan, ICSID Case No. ARB/05/16
48. European Commission (2015) Investment in TTIP and Beyond–The Path For Reform: Enhancing The Right to Regulate and Moving from Current Ad Hoc Arbitration Towards an Investment Court. Brussels
49. Nathalie Bernasconi-Osterwalder (2016) Giving Arbitrators carte blanche–Fair and Equitable Treatment in Investment Treaties In: C. L. Lim (ed), Alternative Visions of the International Law on Foreign Investment: Essays in Honour of Muthucumaraswamy Sornarajah. Cambridge, p 324–346
50. European Union Model BIT Clauses (2023)
51. Methanex Corporation v. United States of America, UNCITRAL

# Chapter 4
# Investment Protection: Investor-State Dispute Settlement

This chapter analyzes the ISDS provisions in China's fourth-generation investment treaties. It first examines the global backlash against investment arbitration and corresponding ISDS reform efforts (Sect. 4.1). Next, it systematically evaluates the ISDS provisions across China's first three generations of investment treaties, tracing their evolution and interpretations in arbitral practice (Sect. 4.2). The chapter then shifts to the emerging fourth generation, arguing that despite notable progress, China's ISDS reform still faces significant challenges. Key aspects include (1) the enhanced ISDS mechanism under recent Chinese investment treaties; (2) China's proposal for ISDS reform at UNCITRAL Working Group III; and (3) China's experience in resolving investor-state disputes (Sect. 4.3).

## 4.1 Investor-State Dispute Settlement Reform

As discussed in Chap. 3, with the increasing number of ISDS cases brought by investors, states realized that old-generation investment treaties—often containing vague and broadly worded provisions—were expansively interpreted by arbitral tribunals, significantly constraining their regulatory space. The criticisms on the ISDS mechanism first gained prominence under the NAFTA in the early 2000s. As a response, three NAFTA contracting states jointly issued an Interpretation Note in 2001 to clarify and reaffirm the meaning of some key treaty provisions [1]. Subsequently, both the US and Canada updated their Model BITs in 2004, aiming to limit tribunals' interpretive discretion while safeguarding greater policy space for states [2–4].

These objectives were primarily achieved in two respects: (1) substantively, the meaning of key treaty provisions was clarified, such as the scope of FET and FPS standards, the criteria for indirect expropriation, and the definition of investment and investor. These clarifications have been comprehensively discussed in Chap. 3; (2)



J. Chao, *The Emerging Fourth Generation of Chinese Investment Treaties*,
https://doi.org/10.1007/978-981-95-5052-4_4

procedurally, the ISDS mechanism was greatly enhanced. For example, the 2004 US Model BIT incorporated several new provisions allowing contracting states to determine certain issues for arbitral tribunals [2, 4]. Furthermore, several issues, including expedited tribunal formation, claim consolidation, and enhanced arbitral transparency, were addressed to promote more fair and efficient dispute resolution proceedings [2, 4].

However, the NAFTA backlash merely marked the beginning of this debate. Subsequently, the criticism of the ISDS mechanism intensified and the backlash against investment arbitration spread worldwide. For instance, Bolivia, Ecuador and Venezuela denounced the ICSID Convention in 2007, 2010 and 2012 respectively and South Africa and Indonesia terminated their investment treaties in 2012 and 2014 respectively [5]. These radical responses essentially constituted a fundamental rejection of the ISDS mechanism.

Notwithstanding these radical responses, two main approaches have been adopted to address the global backlash against investment arbitration. The first approach is to continue to enhance the ISDS mechanism, as demonstrated in the 2018 CPTPP [6]. Specifically, the CPTPP addresses three main aspects of the ISDS mechanism:

(1) Submission of claims to arbitration: CPTPP established a two-step procedure: "consultation and negotiation + submission". The parities need to first undertake consultation and negotiation for six months. If unresolved, the claimant may then submit the disputes under rules such as those of ICSID or UNCITRAL [6]. Also, CPTPP imposes a limitation period of three years and six months [6].
(2) Conduct of arbitration: CPTPP establishes a comprehensive procedural framework to enhance the fairness and efficiency of arbitral proceedings. It provides detailed rules on arbitrator selection, transparency, and claim consolidation. Furthermore, it expands the involvement of contracting states in arbitration, drawing from the 2004 US Model BIT [2, 4, 6]. For example, non-disputing parties may make submissions on treaty interpretation, and arbitral tribunals are required to share draft awards with disputing parties for comment before finalization [6].
(3) Awards: CPTPP explicitly provides that arbitral tribunals can only award monetary damage, applicable interests and restitution (only monetary damage and applicable interests can be awarded in lieu of restitution) [6]. According to Vandevelde, these provisions are designed to safeguard the right of host states to implement regulatory measures, provided that they provide compensation to affected investors when such measures constitute a violation of treaty obligations [4].

It is noteworthy that the 2018 CPTPP evolved from the TPP which had been actively promoted by the US (in January 2017, the Trump Administration formally withdrew the TPP). The ISDS provisions of the 2018 CPTPP are largely modeled on those in the 2012 US Model BIT [6, 7]. However, following its TPP withdrawal, the US changed its position regarding the ISDS mechanism, as demonstrated in the 2018 USMCA. Notably, the USMCA provides that ISDS provisions only apply to Mexico-US investment disputes (Canada does not join) [8]. Furthermore, many limitations are imposed on the ISDS mechanism. For example, the scope of the claim is limited to breach of the national treatment and expropriation and compensation provisions [8]. Also, foreign investors are required to submit the dispute to host state's courts or administrative tribunals and exhaust local remedies before the claim can be brought to arbitration [8]. These limited ISDS provisions have been criticized by many commentators [9], but the US government claims that these provisions ensure foreign investors have "no greater substantive rights" than domestic investors [10].

The second approach is that the EU has proposed an Investment Court System (ICS) to replace the existing ISDS mechanism. So far, the ICS has been included in the EU investment agreements concluded with Canada (the 2016 CETA), Singapore, Vietnam and Chile [11]. As illustrated by the 2016 CETA, the ICS is a two-tiered adjudicative body, including the first instance tribunal and the appellate tribunal [12]:

(1) At the first instance tribunal: like CPTPP, CETA stipulates that investment disputes must first undergo a mandatory consultation period, and if unresolved within 180 days, the disputes then can be submitted to arbitration [6, 12]. Distinctively, CETA introduces an additional procedural requirement that investors should send a notice to the EU for the determination of the respondent [6, 12]. Textual analysis reveals that this determination does not aim to prevent investors from submitting claims [12]. Instead, it serves to identify the proper respondent. Notably, CETA provides that once the respondent has been formally determined, it is barred from subsequently challenging the admissibility of the claim, the jurisdiction of the tribunal, or the validity of the designation [12].

    Furthermore, it should be noted that although the ICS is an adjudicative body, the first instance tribunal is still undertaken under rules such as those of ICSID or UNCITRAL [12]. However, the first instance tribunal should be chosen from fifteen members appointed by the CETA Joint Committee (five from EU, five from Canada, and five from third countries) [12]. Moreover, the CETA lists a set of qualification requirements and ethical rules for members. For example, members are required to have expertise in public international law and desirably in international investment law, international trade law and dispute resolution [12]. Also, members should be independent and avoid conflict of interests [12].
(2) At the appellate tribunal: CETA establishes a broad scope of review for its appellate tribunal. This includes errors of law, manifest errors of fact, and procedural grounds for annulment outlined in Article 52 of the ICSID Convention [12, 13]. Moreover, the CETA Joint Committee would appoint six members for the appellate tribunal (two from EU, two from Canada, and two from third countries) [14]. In addition, these members should also meet the qualification requirements and ethical rules as discussed above [14].

Undoubtedly, the ICS represents an innovative proposal with the potential to fundamentally transform the existing ISDS mechanism. More importantly, according to the EU, it would not only promote the ICS at the bilateral level, but also at the multilateral level—for the establishment of a Multilateral Investment Court (MIC) [15]. The EU contends that the MIC is able to resolve the shortcomings of ad hoc arbitral tribunals in the existing ISDS mechanism [15].

Given the ongoing and intensifying debate surrounding the ISDS mechanism, UNCITRAL established Working Group III in 2017 to explore possible ISDS reforms. Over the past eight years, the Working Group III has achieved some outcomes in terms of individual reforms, such as code of conduct, mediation, and advisory center [16]. Since 2024, the Working Group III has also been working on the draft statutes of a standing mechanism for investment dispute resolution [17–19]. Overall, the ISDS reform remains an ongoing process and still faces substantial challenges.

## 4.2 Investor-State Dispute Settlement Provisions Under the First Three Generations of Chinese Investment Treaties

### *4.2.1 China's Previous Treaty Commitments*

As outlined in Chap. 1, from 1982 to 2007, China's investment treaty practice evolved through three generations, changing from a conservative to a liberal approach. This change was particularly evident in the development of ISDS provisions. This section will first examine the formulation of ISDS provisions under the first three generations and then explore how these ISDS provisions have been interpreted in arbitral practice.

#### 4.2.1.1 China's First and Second-Generation Investment Treaties

With a conservative approach, China's first-generation investment treaties incorporated restrictive ISDS provisions. As exemplified by Chinese Model BIT Version I, they typically permitted international arbitration only for disputes involving the amount of compensation for expropriation, referring all other kinds of disputes to domestic courts [20]. Following its accession to the ICSID in 1990, China's second-generation treaties maintained these restrictive provisions. The key development was the designation of ICSID as the dispute resolution forum, consistent with China's ICSID notification that it would only accept arbitration for disputes over expropriation compensation [21, 22].

#### 4.2.1.2 China's Third-Generation Investment Treaties

Chinese investment treaties entered a liberal third generation in 1998, marked by the adoption of broad ISDS provisions. They permitted all kinds of investment disputes to be submitted to international arbitration, as seen in the Chinese Model BIT Version III [23]. A key feature was the inclusion of "fork-in-the-road" clause, requiring investors to choose between domestic courts and international arbitration (the decision is final and binding). Additionally, these treaties stipulated that at the respondent state's request, investors must first undergo domestic administrative review. Wang explained that this procedural step was designed to provide the host government an opportunity to resolve disputes internally without ultimately restricting investors' access to arbitration [24].

### *4.2.2 Arbitral Tribunals' Treaty Interpretations*

As noted, both first and second generations of Chinese investment treaties only allowed the disputes involving the amount of compensation for expropriation to be submitted to international arbitration. To date, there has been no uniform interpretation of such provisions in arbitral practice. A narrow reading would be that tribunals could determine only the issue of compensation amount, as reflected in *Beijing Shougang and others v. Mongolia* and *AsiaPhos and Norwest v. China* [25, 26]. In contrast, a broad reading would be that tribunals could determine not only the amount issue, but also other issues related to expropriation, as reflected in *Tza Yap Shum v Peru, Sanum Investments v. Laos,* and *Beijing Urban Construction v. Yemen* [27–29].

On this issue, the recent *AsiaPhos and Norwest v. China* case merits particular attention, because for the first time the Chinese government, acting as both respondent and contracting party, expressed its actual intention regarding restrictive ISDS provisions—favoring the narrow reading. Notably, the arbitral tribunal ultimately accepted the Chinese government's position. However, interestingly, one of arbitrators dissented from the majority opinion, advocating instead for the broad reading [26].

Before the discussion of this case, it should be noted that *AsiaPhos and Norwest v. China* was brought based on the 1985 China-Singapore BIT. Its Article 13 provided:

> "2. If the dispute cannot be settled through negotiations within six months, either party to the dispute shall be entitled to submit the dispute to the competent court of the Contracting Party accepting the investment.
>
> *3. If a dispute involving the amount of compensation resulting from expropriation,* nationalization, or other measures having effect equivalent to nationalization or expropriation mentioned in Article 6 cannot be settled within six months … it may be submitted to an international arbitral tribunal established by both parties. *The provisions of this paragraph shall not apply if the national or company concerned has resorted to the procedure specified in the paragraph (2) of this Article*". [30]

Regarding this restrictive ISDS provision, the Chinese government submitted that Article 13(3) was confined to the amount issue and did not extend to other issues such as the occurrence of expropriation and the obligation of compensation [26]. To further clarify, it outlined two distinct procedural paths for investors based on the dispute status: (1) undisputed expropriation: investors could directly submit the amount issue to international arbitration; and (2) disputed expropriation: investors were required to first seek a determination on the occurrence and legality of the expropriation from domestic courts, after which the amount issue could be brought to arbitration [26].

The tribunal accepted the Chinese government's submission, concluding that Article 13(3) was confined to the amount issue and that other issues—the occurrence and legality of the expropriation—fell exclusively within the jurisdiction of domestic courts [26]. The arbitral tribunal further supported its conclusion with the following seven reasons:

First, from the perspective of the ordinary meaning of the arbitration clause, the tribunal favored the decisions rendered by the Court of Appeal of Singapore in *Sanum Investments v. Laos* and the arbitral tribunal in *Beijing Shougang v. Mongolia*, emphasizing that the term "involving" was inherently ambiguous (being neither equivalent to "including" under the broad reading nor to "limited to" under the narrow reading) and must therefore be construed in conjunction with other terms [26]. The tribunal then examined the term "a dispute involving the amount of compensation", stating that the contracting parties' deliberate choice of this term—as opposed to "a dispute involving expropriation"—evidenced their intent to limit arbitrable dispute to the amount issue [26]. Therefore, the ordinary meaning advocated for narrow reading.

Second, from the perspective of the context of the arbitration clause, the tribunal held that Article 6(2) endorsed the narrow reading [26]. Article 6(2) stipulated that, at the investors' request, the legality of the expropriation may be determined by domestic courts [30]. A combined reading of Article 6(2) and Article 13(2)–(3) suggested that they created a framework for "segregated proceedings": (1) the proceedings on the occurrence and legality of the expropriation at domestic courts; and (2) subsequent proceedings on the compensation amount at international tribunal [26].

Third, from the perspective of the "folk-in-the-road" provision, the tribunal held that the second sentence of Article 13(3) was designed to prevent parallel or subsequent proceedings, thereby avoiding contradictory decisions [26]. It further maintained that this "folk-in-the-road" clause was consistent with the narrow reading, because if the investor could submit the legality issue to domestic courts and defer the amount issue to subsequent arbitrations, this clause's objective could be satisfied [26].

Fourth, from the perspective of China's legal framework, the tribunal rejected the claimant's argument that China's domestic courts could not resolve expropriation disputes under international law [26]. On this point, the tribunal held that Article 6(2) clearly allowed domestic courts to review the legality issue [26]. As to whether contracting parties had complied with this obligation, the tribunal found this question fell outside its competence and remained irrelevant for determining the scope of the arbitration clause [26].

Fifth, from the perspective of the treaty's objectives and purposes, the tribunal emphasized that the objective to promote investment does not equate to an intention by contracting states to agree to submit all investment disputes to international arbitration [26]. Consequently, the treaty's objectives and purposes could not serve as a basis for the broad reading.

Sixth, from the perspective of prior case law, the tribunal first distinguished this case from prior jurisprudence, noting that previous tribunals had interpreted either "folk-in-the-road" provisions or provisions similar to Article 6(2), whereas this tribunal was tasked with interpretating both provisions collectively [26]. Despite this, the tribunal carefully reviewed prior decisions and ultimately affirmed that the scope of Article 13(3) was strictly confined to the compensation amount issue [26].

Seventh, from the perspective of the circumstances of the treaty's conclusion, the tribunal found it unnecessary to resort to Article 32 of the Vienna Convention on the Law of Treaties (VCLT), as the interpretation of Article 13(3) was neither ambiguous, obscure, nor manifestly absurd or unreasonable [26, 31]

However, one of arbitrators issued his dissenting opinion, advocating instead for the broad reading. In his reasoning, several points merited attention. First, he empathized that, according to English dictionaries, the meaning of term "involving" was "to include, to contain", and Article 13 therefore should be broadly interpreted [26]. He further explained that if the parties had intended to restrict arbitration to the amount issue, they would have used explicit limiting phrases such as "only/solely" or "limited to" [26].

Second, he mentioned that the "fork-in-the-road" provision was one of conditions for consent to international arbitration—providing that investors were not able to resort to international arbitration if they had already submitted disputes to domestic courts [26]. Under the narrow reading, the arbitration would be restricted to the amount issue. However, it would be difficult to prevent domestic courts from determining the amount issue themselves or prevent governments from submitting the amount issue to domestic courts for determination [26]. Consequently, investors might lose their right to submit claims to arbitration [26].

Third, he stressed that Article 6(1) set out four requirements for legal expropriation, including the requirement that compensation be effectively realizable and provided in a timely manner [26]. Therefore, a domestic court would find it difficult to determine the legality of the expropriation without first assessing if the compensation had been paid in accordance with Article 6(1) [26]. Collectively, these considerations led the tribunal to adopt the narrow reading.

The above discussions reveal the interpretive instability and unpredictability of restrictive ISDS provisions. Notably, many of China's investment arbitration cases have been initiated under its first and second generations of treaties. Consequently, the interpretation of these restrictive ISDS provisions has emerged as a critical issue, essentially determining whether arbitral tribunals have jurisdiction to hear claims.

As to the third generation of Chinse investment treaties, although broad ISDS provisions extend to "any dispute", respondents would still challenge the jurisdiction of arbitral tribunals, particularly by invoking the "fork-in-the-road" provisions, as demonstrated in *Zhongshan Fucheng v. Nigeria* and *Wang v. Finland* [32, 33].

Specifically, *Zhongshan Fucheng v. Nigeria*, brought under the 2001 China-Nigeria BIT, involved a "fork-in-the-road" clause identical to the one found in the 1985 China-Singapore BIT [34]. Nigeria argued that this provision prevented the claimant from bringing this arbitration, because the claimant had resorted to domestic courts [32]. On this point, the tribunal applied two tests developed in *Khan v Mongolia*: (1) the "triple identity test", requiring that domestic court proceedings and treaty arbitration must involve identical parties, causes, and objects; and (2) the "fundamental basis test", requiring that two proceedings fundamentally share the same basis [32]. Ultimately, the tribunal rejected Nigeria's jurisdictional objection, as domestic court proceedings and treaty arbitration in this case involved different parties, different breaches, and different relief sought [32].

Furthermore, *Wang v. Finland*, a case brought under the 2004 China-Finland BIT, also involved a similar "fork-in-the-road" clause [35]. Finland raised a jurisdictional objection, contending that since the claimant had submitted the dispute to its domestic courts and failed to withdraw the case, this clause precluded the arbitral tribunal from exercising jurisdiction [33]. However, the tribunal pointed out that what the claimant sought for was a denial of justice claim, which could not be covered by the "fork-in-the-road" clause [33]. It is only after the claimant had turned to domestic courts and been denied justice that a denial of justice claim might arise [33]. Therefore, the tribunal dismissed Finland's objection [33].

Overall, the tribunals in *Zhongshan Fucheng v. Nigeria* and *Wang v. Finland* both dismissed respondents' jurisdictional objections based on "fork-in-the-road" provisions. Their interpretations would have significant implications for investment arbitration cases initialed under China's third-generation investment treaties.

In addition to the interpretation of ISDS provisions, a common issue across all three generations of treaties is whether Chinese investment treaties apply to the Hong Kong and Macao SARs, as reflected in *Tza Yap Shum v Peru* and *Sanum Investments v. Laos* [27, 28]. In *Tza Yap Shum v Peru,* the claimant was a Hong Kong resident who brought claims under the 1994 China-Peru BIT. The tribunal did not directly address the territorial application issue. Instead, it focused on determining whether the claimant could submit the investment dispute to arbitration under the ICSID Convention and the 1994 China-Peru BIT [27].

Specially, the 1994 China-Peru BIT defined "investors" as "natural persons who have nationality of the People's Republic of China in accordance with its laws" [22]. The tribunal referred to the Nationality Act of the People's Republic of China, which applied to Hong Kong SAR, and noted that Chinese nationality was conferred on "natural persons of Chinese descent born in Chinese territory" [27]. The claimant's passport indicated he was born in the Fuji Province to Chinese parents, leading the tribunal to conclude that he held Chinese nationality [27]. Furthermore, the ICSID Convention required the tribunal to verify the claimant's Chinese nationality. Since the 1994 China-Peru BIT did not explicitly exclude Chinese nationals residing in Hong Kong, the tribunal ultimately held that the claimant was entitled to protection under the treaty [27].

Chen criticized that the tribunal ignored the unique relationship between China and Hong Kong SAR [36]. He argued that the 1994 China-Peru BIT was concluded before Hong Kong's handover in 1997 and did not satisfy the requirements under the Sino-British Joint Declaration and the Hong Kong Basic Law for the extension of Chinese treaties to Hong Kong SAR, so the 1994 China-Peru BIT did not apply to Hong Kong SAR and the claimant was not entitled to submit the dispute under the treaty [36]. However, given that both the ICSID convention and the 1994 China-Peru BIT defined "nationality" as the sole requirement for "investors"—with no additional requirements such as "residence"—the tribunal's decision on this issue could be considered reasonable [37].

In contrast, the territorial application issue was directly addressed in *Sanum Investments v. Laos* [28, 38, 39]. This case was brought by a Macao-based company under the 1993 China-Laos BIT. On 13 December 2013, the tribunal delivered its Award on Jurisdiction concluding that the 1993 China-Laos BIT applied to the Macao SAR [28]. In January 2014, Laos filed an application to the Singapore High Court with two diplomatic letters. In the first letter, the Lao government noted that this 1993 BIT did not extend to Macao. This position was later confirmed by the Chinese Embassy in Laos in the second letter, which stipulated that any future application would be subject to a separate arrangement between the two governments [38]. On 20 January 2015, the Singapore High Court rendered its judgment accepting Laos' application [38]. However, the High Court's judgment was subsequently turned over by the Singapore Court of Appeal on 29 September 2016 [39].

Regarding the territorial application issues, the Singapore Court of Appeal applied Article 15 of the Vienna Convention on the Succession of States in respect of Treaties and the VCLT Article 29—the "moving treaty frontier" rule [39]. This principle suggests that the 1993 China-Laos BIT would presumptively apply to China's entire territory, including the Macao SAR. For Laos to argue that the treaty did not extend to Macao, it must demonstrate either (a) that the BIT itself reflected an intention to exclude Macao; or (b) that other evidence conclusively established the BIT's inapplicability to Macao [39].

For the first exception, the 1993 China-Laos BIT was silent on territorial applicability [39]. For the second exception, the Singapore Court of Appeal examined several pieces of evidence, including the 1987 Sino-Portugal Joint Declaration, Hong Kong experience, 1999 UN Secretary-General Note, 2001 WTO report and 2014 diplomatic letters [39]. The Court applied the critical date doctrine and categorized two diplomatic letters as post-critical date evidence [39]. The Court further noted that since all pre-critical date evidence failed to displace the "moving treaty frontier" rule, these two diplomatic letters, being post-critical date evidence, attempted to contradict this established position and were therefore accorded no weight [39].

The judgment of Singapore Court of Appeal drew strong criticism from the Chinese government. A spokesperson for China's Foreign Ministry denounced that the Singaporean court's ruling was incorrect on this point, as China had twice confirmed that this 1993 BIT does not apply to Macao SAR [40]. Meanwhile, Xu, the Director-General of China's Department of Treaty and Law, published an article on Legal Daily explaining China's treaty arrangements concerning the Hong Kong and Macao SARs [41].

Regarding China's arrangement for the Hong Kong and Macao SARs, it is important to first note that China does not accept the moving treaty frontier rules. In China's view, the treaties ceding sovereignty over Hong Kong and Macao were "unequal treaties" and thus "null and void" [42]. As for the handovers of Hong Kong and Macao, China maintains that there was no transfer of sovereignty [42]. Under the

Sino-Britain Joint Declaration, China declares the "resumption" of sovereignty while the UK declares "restoration" [42, 43]. For Macao, both Portugal and China use the term "resumption" [42, 44]. Therefore, the treaty succession rules do not apply in these cases.

Instead, China, Britain and Portugal made special arrangements for Hong Kong and Macao. Specifically, the Hong Kong and Macao SARs have the authority to conclude treaties independently. For example, the Sino-Portuguese Joint Declaration authorizes the Macao SAR to conclude treaties in economic, technical and cultural fields in its own name [44]. A similar provision is found in the Sino-Britain Joint Declaration regarding Hong Kong [43].

Second, Chinese treaties may be extended to the Hong Kong and Macao SARs under specific conditions. For example, the Sino-Portuguese Joint Declaration stipulates that the Central Government decides on the application of Chinese treaties to the Macao SAR after assessing the circumstances and needs, and consulting the SAR government [44]. It further provides that the agreements to which China is not a party but which are implemented in the SAR may remain in force [44]. Similar provisions are found in the Sino-Britain Joint Declaration regarding Hong Kong [43]. These special arrangements are also incorporated in the Hong Kong and Macao Basic Laws [45, 46].

Third, the Chinese government had already submitted two diplomatic notes to the UN Secretary-General on 20 June 1997 and 13 December 1999, accompanied by lists of 214 and 158 treaties that would remain applicable to these two SARs respectively after their handovers [47]. Article IV of the notes stipulated that any additional treaties extending to Hong Kong or Macao would require separate arrangements [47]. Given that copies of these notes were circulated to all UN states, Xu argued that these special arrangements for Hong Kong and Macao gained widespread international acceptance [41].

Therefore, as a general rule, Chinese investment treaties do not extend to the Hong Kong and Macao SARs. Any extension is conditional upon a decision by the central government after consulting SAR governments and the other treaty party [40]. In *Sanum Investments v. Laos*, the Singapore Court of Appeal appeared to misinterpret these special arrangements. Lim argued that the carefully drafted settlements among China, Britain and Portugal "have been misunderstood, even questioned" in the field of investment arbitration [42].

Regarding the territorial application issue, it is also noteworthy that at least two Chinese investment treaties—treaties with Russia and Mexico—expressly exclude the Hong Kong and Macao SARs from the treaty scope [48, 49]. Xu explained that the Chinese central government would not expressly state that Chinese investment treaties do not apply to the Hong Kong and Macao SARs, as other contracting parties would generally share an understanding of this principle [41]. During treaty negotiations, if counterparties expressed uncertainty about the treaties' applicability to the Hong Kong and Macao SARs, the Chinese government would clarify its position by invoking the Hong Kong and Macao Basic Laws and relevant regulations [41]. Only in exceptional cases—and solely at the request of the other contracting party—would China explicitly exclude the SARs from treaty application to reaffirm its stance [41].

Nevertheless, textual silence has resulted in some "uncertainty and confusion" [42]. The *Sanum Investments v. Laos* case demonstrates that the public does not fully understand China's special arrangements for the Hong Kong and Macao SARs [41]. This suggests a need for further clarification of China's position [42]. The fourth generation of Chinese investment treaties could serve as an ideal platform to incorporate an express provision confirming this policy. For the existing Chinese investment treaties, the Chinese government might consider issuing diplomatic notes to its treaty partners as a clarification mechanism [42].

## 4.3 Investor-State Dispute Settlement Reform Under the Fourth Generation of Chinese Investment Treaties

As stated in Chap. 3, since 2008, Chinese investment treaties have promoted a more balanced approach between the protection of foreign investment and the right of states to regulate through both substantive and procedural provisions. While the Sect. 3.3 provided a comprehensive analysis of balanced substantive provisions, this section will focus specifically on China's balancing practice in ISDS provisions.

China's ISDS balancing practice has evolved through two distinct phases: (1) from 2008 to 2015, China progressively refined ISDS provisions for promoting a more comprehensive and balanced mechanism. This development largely aligned with the first approach to addressing the global backlash against investment arbitration, as previously outlined; (2) after 2015, due to ongoing ISDS debates and divergent reform proposals, China has fundamentally reconsidered the ISDS mechanism, as reflected in its reform proposal submitted to UNCITRAL Working Group III in 2019. The following analysis will examine these two developmental stages in detail.

### *4.3.1 Refined ISDS Provisions in Recent Chinese Investment Treaties*

An example of China's progressive refinement of ISDS provisions can be found in the 2012 China-Canada BIT. A detailed analysis reveals that this BIT enhances the ISDS mechanism in three key aspects:

First, similar to CPTPP, the China-Canada BIT requires disputing parties to initiate consultations after submitting a notice of intent to seek an amicable settlement [6, 50]. Furthermore, the treaty stipulates that disputes may be submitted only within a specific timeframe: no earlier than six months after the triggering event, and no later than three years from investors' knowledge of the alleged breach [50]. Once these procedural conditions are satisfied, the claim could be submitted under the rules such as those of ICSID or UNCITRAL [50].

Second, similar to CPTPP, the China-Canada BIT enhances the engagement of contracting parties in arbitral proceedings [6, 50]. For example, the treaty allows the non-disputing party to receive case documents, attend hearings, and make submissions on treaty interpretation [50]. More importantly, it establishes that a joint interpretation by the contracting parties is binding on the arbitral tribunal [50]. Furthermore, it further enhances procedural fairness and efficiency through rules on claim consolidation, third party, arbitrators, and transparency [50].

Third, the China-Canada BIT further stipulates that final awards may only impose monetary damage and applicable interests [50]. As noted, these provisions aim to preserve the contracting states' regulatory autonomy while ensuring compensation for investors affected by measures that breach treaty obligations. Furthermore, the treaty requires all awards to be made publicly available [50]. The publication of other documents and the opening of hearings shall be determined by the disputing party [50].

While the ISDS provisions in the 2012 China-Canada BIT are comprehensive, several issues remain unresolved, such as the transparency of arbitral proceedings. The transparency issue was first raised in NAFTA ISDS practice. As a response, the three NAFTA contracting states issued an Interpretation Note advocating for public access to documents [1]. This trend was subsequently reinforced by transparency requirements in the 2004 and 2012 US Model BITs and the entry into force of the UNCITRAL Rules on Transparency in Treaty-based Investor-State Arbitration (UNCITRAL Transparency Rules) in 2014 [2, 7, 51]. Given that the 2015 China-Australia FTA has incorporated provisions modeled on UNCITRAL Transparency Rules [51–53], it is suggested that China uphold similar transparency standards in its fourth-generation investment treaties.

Another issue is related to appellate mechanism. The appellate mechanism was first promoted by the US in its 2012 Model BIT [7]. China did not address this issue until the 2015 China-Australia FTA, mandating negotiations to establish an appellate mechanism for reviewing awards on questions of law [52]. As discussed later, China further elaborated on its design in its reform proposal at the UNCITRAL in 2019.

### 4.3.2 *China's Proposal for ISDS Reform at UNCITRAL*

As noted, UNCTRAL established Working Group III in 2017 to focus specifically on the ISDS reform. In recent years, China has actively participated in the Working Group's reform efforts. First, in its 2017 submission, China indicated that it was still evaluating ISDS reform options, noting the need to strike a proper balance between investment protection and the right of states to regulate [54]. Subsequently, in its 2019 reform proposal, China expressed skepticism about ad hoc arbitral tribunals, citing concerns regarding error correction, award predictability, arbitrator independence, third-party funding regulation, as well as time and cost efficiency [55].

Consequently, China proposed establishing a permanent multilateral appellate mechanism to address these shortcomings in the existing ISDS system [55]. China suggested that this multilateral appellate mechanism could be modeled on the WTO dispute settlement system, serving as a complement to the current investment arbitration system [55]. Additionally, China emphasized that parties' right to appoint arbitrators should be preserved as the essential aspect of arbitration [55].

Setting aside the debate on whether it is necessary to ensure consistency in arbitral awards and whether establishing an appellate mechanism can achieve this goal [5], international community may find this "hybrid" approach confusing, because the WTO provides a system of international adjudication and this hybrid approach would graft an adjudicative appellate mechanism onto international arbitration. For example, Roberts and St John augured that China's "hybrid ISDS/AB approach" likely reflected a compromise among internal governmental viewpoints, one that could evolve in the future [56].

However, a closer examination reveals that this hybrid approach is, in fact, rooted in China's domestic arbitration system. In China, domestic arbitration gives prominence to documents and seldom uses factual witnesses and expert witnesses. On average, the arbitration process takes less than one year. Moreover, arbitral tribunals need to submit draft awards to Chinese arbitral institutions for scrutiny before signing the awards. Although Chinese arbitral institutions emphasize that the independence of arbitral tribunals is not affected, these institutions play a role in correcting errors to some extent [57]. In contrast, international arbitration is a transparent process requiring the parties to disclose their positions. Furthermore, arbitral tribunals provide detailed awards, and international arbitral institutions only administer proceedings. Therefore, China's policymakers and international community have different perceptions of how to arbitrate, and China's hybrid approach, drawing on experience from domestic arbitration, is distinguished from the general perception of international arbitration.

After 2019, both the 2020 RCEP and the 2020 CAI deferred the ISDS provisions for future negotiations [58, 59]. In the CAI negotiations, a key issue will be the compatibility between China's "hybrid ISDS/AB approach" and the EU's two-tiered adjudicative body. Notably, China's reform proposal explicitly emphasized the parties' right to appoint arbitrators—a stance that significantly diverges from the EU's Tribunal with fifteen appointed Members. This divergence has drawn attention from scholars such as Roberts and St John, who questioned whether China would adopt its usual flexible approach to collaborate with the EU on ISDS reform [56]. The outcome of these negotiations remains uncertain.

### *4.3.3 China's Experience in Resolving Investor-State Disputes*

The above analysis demonstrates that, against the backdrop of ongoing ISDS debates, China's fourth-generation investment treaties continue to face significant challenges in reforming the ISDS mechanism. To explore viable solutions, China may draw on its own experience in resolving investor-state disputes.

Firstly, as outlined in Chap. 1, there have been 28 cases brought under Chinese investment treaties to date, 20 of which were brought by Chinese investors. A closer examination reveals that most of these cases involved Chinese SOEs or large companies and primarily concerned energy and construction disputes relating to China's BRI. Consequently, Chinese investors have increasingly relied on the ISDS mechanism to protect their overseas investments. However, as previously discussed, many of these cases have stalled at the jurisdiction stage due to restrictive ISDS provisions. This has led to calls for China to modernize its investment treaty network to enhance protection for its overseas investments.

Second, as China's Going Global Strategy and the BRI advance and as a growing number of Chinese investors expand abroad, China should take a more proactive stance in promoting ISDS reform. Such efforts would contribute to establishing an international consensus on a more effective and predictable ISDS mechanism. As stated earlier, post-2019 Chinese investment treaties such as the 2020 RCEP and the 2020 CAI deferred ISDS provisions for future negotiations, reflecting divergent views among states on this issue [58, 59]. While China submitted an ISDS reform proposal to UNCITRAL, its hybrid approach differed from the conventional perception of international arbitration. Therefore, China may need to reassess and refine its reform proposal.

Third, regarding the refinement of reform proposals, it is advisable for Chinese policymakers to engage in discussions with Chinese companies and international arbitration lawyers. As observed, Chinese companies have become significant participants in investment arbitration. Moreover, in recent years, Chinese lawyers have played an increasingly active role in this field—serving as legal counsel, publishing scholarly articles, and organizing conferences and seminars. Given this growing expertise, it would be beneficial for China's policymakers, companies, and lawyers to share insights and practical experiences. In fact, in October 2024, an UNCITRAL intersessional meeting was held in Chengdu, China, for discussing the key issues of the appellate mechanism [60]. Such discussion could help China formulate more widely accepted ISDS reform proposals.

## 4.4 Conclusion

In the first three generations, Chinese investment treaties shifted from a conservative to a liberal approach in their ISDS provisions. However, two critical interpretative issues have emerged in arbitral practice: (1) the restrictive ISDS provisions in the first and second generations have been subject to two conflicting interpretations—a broad reading and a narrow reading—leaving many of China's investment arbitration cases entangled in jurisdictional disputes; and (2) China's special arrangements for the Hong Kong and Macao SARs have been misunderstood, creating uncertainty and confusion regarding the territorial application of Chinese investment treaties.

In the fourth-generation treaties, although China has increasingly refined the ISDS provisions and submitted its ISDS reform proposal at UNCITRAL, it still faces significant challenges in reforming the ISDS mechanism. Given the growing number of Chinese companies expanding abroad, China should take a more proactive stance in promoting ISDS reform. Additionally, China's policymakers are advised to draw on the experience of Chinese companies and arbitration lawyers to develop more widely accepted reform proposals. Accelerating these reforms will be crucial in ensuring stability and predictability in resolving future investment disputes.

## References


1. NAFTA Free Trade Commission Notes of Interpretation of Certain Chapter 11 Provisions (2001)
2. United States Model BIT (2004)
3. Canada Model BIT (2004)
4. Kenneth. J. Vandevelde (2009) A Comparison of the 2004 and 1994 U.S. Model BITs: Rebalancing Investor and Host Country Interests. In: Karl. P. Sauvant (ed), Yearbook on International Investment Law & Policy 2008–2009. Oxford, p 283–316
5. Chin Leng Lim (2020) Reaching for Utopia, Geneva as Inspiration for Investment Disputes?. In: Meredith Kolsky Lewis, Junji Nakagawa, Rostam J. Neuwirth, Colin B. Picker, and Peter-Tobias Stoll (ed) A Post-WTO International Legal Order Utopian, Dystopian and Other Scenarios. Springer, Switzerland, pp. 167–185
6. Comprehensive and Progressive Agreement for Trans-Pacific Partnership (2018)
7. United States Model BIT (2012)
8. United States-Mexico-Canada Agreement (2018)
9. Giorgio Sacerdoti (2020) Is USMCA really "the new gold standard" of investment protection?. Columbia FDI Perspective No. 281. https://ccsi.columbia.edu/sites/ccsi.columbia.edu/files/content/docs/publications/No%20281%20-%20FINAL%20-%20Sacerdoti.pdf. Accessed 11 August 2025
10. United States Trade Representative (2017) Summary of Objectives for the NAFTA Renegotiation. https://ustr.gov/sites/default/files/files/Press/Releases/NAFTAObjectives.pdf. Accessed 11 August 2025
11. European Commission, Guide to Investment Court System. https://webgate.acceptance.ec.europa.eu/portal9/en/content/guide-investment-court-system. Accessed 11 August 2025
12. EU-Canada Comprehensive Economic and Trade Agreement (2016)
13. ICSID Convention (1966)
14. Decision No 1/2021 Of the CETA Joint Committee of 29 January 2021 Setting Out the Administrative and Organisational Matters Regarding the Functioning of the Appellate Tribunal [2021/264] (2021)
15. European Commission, Multilateral Investment Court Project. https://policy.trade.ec.europa.eu/enforcement-and-protection/multilateral-investment-court-project_en. Accessed 11 August 2025
16. Anthea Roberts and Taylor St John (2023) UNCITRAL and ISDS Reform: Moving to the Delivery Phase. Blog of the European Journal of International Law. https://www.ejiltalk.org/uncitral-and-isds-reform-moving-to-the-delivery-phase/. Accessed 11 August 2025
17. UNCITRAL Working Group III (2024) A/CN.9/WG.III/WP.239—Possible reform of investor-State dispute settlement (ISDS): Draft statute of a standing mechanism for the resolution of international investment disputes. https://docs.un.org/en/A/CN.9/WG.III/WP.239. Accessed 11 August 2025

18. UNCITRAL Working Group III (2024) A/CN.9/WG.III/WP.249—Summary of the intersessional meeting on investor-State dispute settlement (ISDS) reform submitted by the Government of the People's Republic of China. https://docs.un.org/en/A/CN.9/WG.III/WP.249. Accessed 11 August 2025
19. UNCITRAL Working Group III (2025) A/CN.9/WG.III/WP.256—Possible reform of investor-State dispute settlement (ISDS): Structure and design of a standing mechanism for the resolution of international investment disputes. https://docs.un.org/en/A/CN.9/WG.III/WP.256. Accessed 11 August 2025
20. Chinese Model BIT Version I (1984)
21. ICSID (2024) Contracting States and Measures Taken by Them for the Purpose of the Convention. https://icsid.worldbank.org/sites/default/files/ICSID%203/2024%20-%20Aug%2025%20-%20ICSID%208.pdf. Accessed 11 August 2025
22. China-Peru BIT (1994)
23. Chinese Model BIT Version III (1997)
24. Guiguo Wang (2011) Investor-State Dispute Settlement in China. Transnational Dispute Settlement 5
25. Beijing Shougang and others v. Mongolia, PCA Case No. 2010-20
26. AsiaPhos Limited and Norwest Chemicals Pte Ltd v. People's Republic of China, ICSID Case No. ADM/21/1: Award of the Tribunal and Dissenting Opinion by Stanimir Alexandrov (16 February 2023)
27. Señor Tza Yap Shum v. The Republic of Peru, ICSID Case No. ARB/07/6
28. Sanum Investments v. Lao People's Democratic Republic, PCA Case No. 2013–13, Award on Jurisdiction (13 December 2013)
29. Beijing Urban Construction Group Co. Ltd. v. Republic of Yemen, ICSID Case No. ARB/14/30
30. China-Singapore BIT (1985)
31. Vienna Convention on the Law of Treaties (1969)
32. Zhongshan Fucheng Industrial Investment Co. Ltd. v. Federal Republic of Nigeria (ad hoc)
33. Wang Jiazhu v. Republic of Finland (2013 UNCITRAL Arbitration Rules)
34. China–Nigeria BIT (2001)
35. China–Finland BIT (2004)
36. An Chen (2009) Queries to the Recent ICSID Decision on Jurisdiction Upon the Case of Tza Yap Shum v. Republic of Peru: Should China-Peru BIT 1994 be Applied to Hong Kong SAR under the "One Country Two systems" Policy?. Journal of World Investment & Trade, Volume 10, Issue 6: 337–372
37. Wei Shen (2011) The Good, the Bad or the Ugly? A Critique of the Decision on Jurisdiction and Competence in Tza Yap Shum v. The Republic of Peru. Chinese Journal of International Law, Volume 10: 55–95
38. Sanum Investments v. Lao People's Democratic Republic, Judgment of the High Court of Singapore [2015] SGHC 15 (20 January 2015)
39. Sanum Investments v. Lao People's Democratic Republic, Judgment of the Court of Appeal of Singapore [2016] SGCA 57 (29 September 2016)
40. China's Ministry of Foreign Affairs (2016) Foreign Ministry Spokesperson Hua Chunying's Regular Press Conference on October 21, 2016. https://www.italaw.com/sites/default/files/case-documents/italaw7687.pdf. Accessed 12 August 2025
41. Hong Xu (2016) The Application of International Treaties to the Hong Kong and Macao Special Administrative Regions. Legal Daily (in Chinese: Guo Ji Tiao Yue Shi Yong Xiang Gang He Ao Men Te Qu De Shi Jian)
42. Chin Leng Lim (2018) Fragrant Harbour and Oyster Mirror: Beijing's Treaty Policy toward Hong Kong and Macao. In: Lisa E. Sachs and Lise Johnson (ed) Yearbook on International Investment Law & Policy 2015–2016. Oxford, pp. 375–411
43. The Joint Declaration of the Government of the United Kingdom of Great Britain and Northern Ireland and the Government of the People's Republic of China on the Question of Hong Kong (1984)

44. The Sino-Portuguese Joint Declaration on the Question of Macao (1987)
45. The Basic Law of the Hong Kong Special Administrative Region of the People's Republic of China (1997)
46. The Basic Law of the Macao Special Administrative Region of the People's Republic of China (1999)
47. United Nations, Multilateral Treaties Deposited with the Secretary-General. https://treaties.un.org/pages/historicalinfo.aspx#China. Accessed 12 August 2025
48. China-Russia BIT (2006)
49. China-Mexico BIT (2008)
50. China-Canada BIT (2012)
51. UNCITRAL Rules on Transparency in Treaty-based Investor-State Arbitration (2014)
52. China-Australia FTA (2015)
53. UNCITRAL, Status: UNCITRAL Rules on Transparency in Treaty-based Investor-State Arbitration. https://uncitral.un.org/en/texts/arbitration/conventions/foreign_arbitral_awards/status. Accessed 12 August 2025
54. UNCITRAL (2017) A/CN.9/918/Add.1 Settlement of Commercial Disputes Investor-State Dispute Settlement Framework: Compilation of Comments. https://documents.un.org/doc/undoc/gen/v17/005/13/pdf/v1700513.pdf?OpenElement. Accessed 12 August 2025
55. UNCITRAL (2019) A/CN.9/WG.III/WP.177 Possible Reform of Investor-State Dispute Settlement (ISDS): Submission from the Government of China. https://docs.un.org/en/A/CN.9/WG.III/WP.177. Accessed 12 August 2025
56. Anthea Roberts and Taylor St John (2019) UNCITRAL and ISDS Reform: China's Proposal. Blog of the European Journal of International Law. https://www.ejiltalk.org/uncitral-and-isds-reform-chinas-proposal/. Accessed 12 August 2025
57. China International Economic and Trade Arbitration Commission (CIETAC) Arbitration Rules (2024)
58. Regional Comprehensive Economic Partnership (2020)
59. China-EU Comprehensive Agreement on Investment (2020)
60. UNCITRAL (2024) A/CN.9/WG.III/WP.249 Summary of the Intersessional Meeting on Investor-State Dispute Settlement (ISDS) Reform Submitted by the Government of the People's Republic of China. https://docs.un.org/en/A/CN.9/WG.III/WP.249. Accessed 12 August 2025

# Chapter 5
# Towards the Fourth Generation of Chinese Investment Treaties

The previous discussions demonstrate that China's fourth-generation investment treaties have emerged, characterized by a liberal approach to investment liberalization and a balanced approach to investment protection. This chapter first summarizes the key features of these fourth-generation treaties (Sect. 5.1) and then analyzes their driving factors (Sect. 5.2). Finally, it argues that, through these four generations of treaties, China has established a comprehensive investment treaty network at the bilateral, regional and multilateral levels (Sect. 5.3).

## 5.1 The Emergence of the Fourth Generation of Chinese Investment Treaties

As previously discussed, Chinese investment treaties concluded between 1982 to 2007 can be classified into three distinct generations: (1) 1982–1989, (2) 1990–1997, and (3) 1998–2007 [1]. These three generations primarily emphasized investment protection, with their approaches evolving from conservative to liberal. In contrast, the fourth generation of Chinese investment treaties, emerging post-2008, is built on two fundamental pillars: (1) the promotion of investment liberalization; and (2) the balance between investment protection and the right of states to regulate. The key features of these generational shifts have been outlined in Table 5.1.

More specifically, in promoting investment liberalization, China's fourth-generation investment treaties have primarily accepted the pre-establishment national treatment and negative list approach. This represents a paradigm shift in China's foreign investment regulatory regime, as evidenced by the 2019 New Foreign Investment Law. In addition, these treaties have addressed other liberalization issues, including absolute market access obligations, SOE disciplines, performance requirement prohibitions, regulatory transparency, environmental protection, labor rights, corporate social responsibility, as well as investment facilitation. Not only is the scope

 
J. Chao, *The Emerging Fourth Generation of Chinese Investment Treaties*,
https://doi.org/10.1007/978-981-95-5052-4_5

**Table 5.1** Key characteristics of China's four generations of investment treaties

| | 1st G | 2nd G | 3rd G | 4th G |
|---|---|---|---|---|
| Period | 1982–1989 | 1990–1997 | 1998–2007 | 2008-present |
| Protection | Conservative | Conservative | Liberal | Balanced |
| Liberalization | Not Addressed | | | Liberal |

remarkably comprehensive, but China has also undertaken substantial commitments in each of these critical areas.

Furthermore, China's fourth-generation investment treaties have balanced investment protection with the right of states to regulate by refining substantive and procedural provisions. On the substantive level, these treaties primary focus on two aspects: (1) clarifying key provisions—such as the definitions of investment and investor, national treatment, MFN treatment, FET and FPS standards and indirect expropriation—to prevent expansive interpretations by arbitral tribunals; and (2) incorporating new exception clauses to preserve host states' regulatory space in areas including essential security, environmental protection, prudential and monetary policy.

Nevertheless, China's balancing practice exhibits certain inconsistencies. Given that the current balancing approach draws upon established investment arbitration jurisprudence and aligns with UNCTAD's reform recommendations [2], it is advisable for China to maintain this balanced approach in its future treaty practice. It is also advisable for China to further address two critical issues: (1) the explicit inclusion of SOEs under the definition of investor; and (2) the treatment of investors' legitimate expectations under the FET standard. These issues respond to China's investment arbitration cases and align with contemporary trends in investment treaty practice, respectively.

On the procedural level, China's balancing practice has evolved through two distinct phases: (1) from 2008 to 2015, China's fourth-generation investment treaties progressively refined the ISDS provisions to promote a comprehensive and balanced dispute resolution framework; and (2) since 2015, in light of ongoing ISDS debates and divergent reform proposals, China has conducted a fundamental reassessment of the existing ISDS mechanism. In 2019, it submitted a proposal for ISDS reform at the UNCITRAL Working Group III, advocating for establishing a WTO-style multilateral appellate mechanism to complement the existing investment arbitration system [3]. A closer examination reveals that this hybrid approach was rooted in China's domestic arbitration practices, thereby diverging from conventional perception of international arbitration. This helps explain why this approach generated significant confusion within the international community [4]. Given the growing involvement of Chinese companies and lawyers in investment arbitration in recent years, China's policymakers are advised to engage in discussion with them. Drawing on their practical experience could help formulate more widely accepted reform proposals, thereby accelerating and completing the fourth-generation ISDS reform.

In addition, one issue emerging from China's investment arbitration cases warrants attention—whether Chinese investment treaties apply to the Hong Kong and Macao

SARs. As discussed, upon the handovers of Hong Kong and Macao, China already established special arrangements with Britain and Portugal, setting forth the general principle that Chinese investment treaties do not automatically extend to the Hong Kong and Macao SARs unless the Chinese Central government—after consulting the views of SAR governments—explicitly determines otherwise. However, this principle has been misunderstood in investment arbitration, creating uncertainty and confusion regarding the territorial application of Chinese investment treaties. Therefore, the fourth generation of Chinese investment treaties could serve as an ideal platform to incorporate an express provision confirming this policy.

Overall, the development of China's fourth-generation investment treaties has been a gradual and ongoing process. This evolution, which began in 2008, has spanned over 17 years. To date, while these treaties have made significant progress in promoting investment liberalization and balancing investment protection with the right of states to regulate, certain challenges remain—especially regarding ISDS reform.

As discussed in Chap. 1, the fourth generation's evolution differs markedly from that of its predecessors. China's first three treaty generations were characterized by clear turning points, after which each generation largely maintain a consistent framework. This pattern emerged because China's earlier approach essentially involved a step-by-step adoption of the then-prevailing liberal investment treaty model. However, the current landscape has shifted significantly. Today, no consensus exists regarding the future direction of investment treaty making. Amid the global backlash against investment arbitration, numerous countries—including China—have been actively exploring appropriate reform approaches. This explains why the fourth generation's development remains a gradual and ongoing process.

The following section examines the driving factors behind China's fourth-generation investment treaties, shedding light on both their emergence and their progressive evolution.

## 5.2 The Driving Factors Behind the Fourth Generation of Chinese Investment Treaties

### *5.2.1 The Changing Landscape of International Investment Treaties*

As discussed, the modern investment treaty regime emerged from a unique historical, economic, and social context. Initially, these treaties were designed primarily to protect foreign investors and were predominantly concluded between developed and developing countries. The bilateral approach stemmed from divergent views on standards of expropriation and compensation [5]. These objectives were typically reflected in treaty preambles. For example, the first investment treaty—the 1959 Germany-Pakistan BIT—stated in its preamble that this agreement aimed to "create favourable conditions for [foreign] investments" in order to "promote investment, encourage private industrial and financial enterprise and to increase the prosperity of both the States" [6]. Similar objective was subsequently incorporated into later BITs, including all three versions of Chinese Model BIT [7–9], and was eventually invoked by arbitral tribunals to justify expansive interpretations of treaty provisions.

Regarding expansive treaty interpretations, the core problem lay in permitting foreign investors to challenge host states' regulatory space—particularly concerning environmental protection, energy, and public health [10]. Criticisms of ISDS grew increasingly severe, ultimately triggering the NAFTA backlash and subsequent global backlash against investment arbitration. Under the NAFAT backlash, the US updated its Model BIT in 2004 with two main objectives: (1) reducing the discretion of arbitral tribunals while preserving states' regulatory space for legitimate public policy objectives [11]; and (2) reconciling BITs with FTAs, thereby substantially promoting investment market liberalization [12]. The core liberalization provision was pre-establishment national treatment, while other provisions were introduced to address regulatory transparency, environmental protection and labor rights [12].

Subsequently, the EU—having gained treaty-making power through the Lisbon Treaty—has established its new international investment policy based on three key pillars: (1) investment protection: the EU emphasizes the need to attract and protect international investment while preserving states' right to regulate for legitimate public policy objectives11; (2) investment liberalization: the EU aims to "level the playing field for foreign investors on third country markets" [11]. To achieve this, the EU goes beyond pre-establishment national treatment to promote absolute market accesses rules and SOE disciplines that prevent discrimination against foreign investors [13]. Meanwhile, the EU expands the treaty scope to include corporate social responsibility and climate change—grouping these provisions with environmental protection and labor rights under the overarching sustainable development objective [14]; and (3) investment facilitation: the EU seeks to simplify the establishment, operation, and expansion of foreign investments through measures such as streamlining administrative procedures, publishing investment-related laws and regulations, and providing relevant information [11].

The investment policies and practices of the US and EU have exerted significant influence on contemporary mega-FTAs, including the 2018 CPTPP, 2020 RCEP, and 2020 CAI [13, 15, 16]. This evolution reflects a growing recognition among states that the objectives of investment treaties have shifted from solely investment protection to encompassing investment protection, liberalization, and facilitation. Notably, investment protection and liberalization provisions have dominated treaty texts through comprehensive and detailed clauses, whereas investment facilitation has primarily progressed at the WTO—particularly 2024 IFD agreement, which currently boasts the participation of 127 members [17, 18].

This evolving global landscape has profoundly shaped China's fourth-generation investment treaties. In particular, the fourth generation has been developed under the China-US and China-EU BIT negotiations. Therefore, unlike the first three generations exclusively focusing on investment protection, the fourth generation systematically incorporates both investment protection and liberalization.

### 5.2.2 *The Balance Between Investment Protection and the Right of States to Regulate*

As discussed previously, numerous countries—including the US, the EU, China—have balanced investment protection with the right of states to regulate in investment treaties. The balancing practice has been undertaken both substantially and procedurally. In either case, the reform is still ongoing and faces significant challenges.

Regarding substantive protection provisions, an international consensus has emerged among states that their regulatory space should be preserved for legitimate public policy objectives [2]. However, states have held divergent views on the extent to which their right to regulate should be balanced against investment protection. This divergence has been reflected in their different balancing practices. In 2020, UNCTAD analyzed the balanced approaches adopted by recent investment treaties and formulated a set of actions to accelerate investment treaty reforms [2]. Specifically, UNCTAD focused on eight key treaty provisions, including the definitions of investment and investor, FET and FPS standards, indirect expropriation, and so on. In its analysis, each provision had multiple reform actions, and even under the same reform action, different states adopted varying wording [2].

In contrast, the ISDS reform has faced greater challenges. As discussed in Chap. 4, under the global backlash against investment arbitration, the first question is whether to retain the ISDS mechanism. Bolivia, Ecuador and Venezuela, South Africa, and Indonesia have expressed serious resistance to the ISDS mechanism [19]. Assuming the answer is affirmative, the second question arises: how to reform the existing ISDS mechanism. Significant divergences persist, and reform approaches mainly include: (1) selectively adopting the ISDS mechanism (e.g., the 2018 USMCA, which only apply to US-Mexico disputes [20]); (2) refining the existing ISDS mechanism (such as improving arbitral proceedings and regulating arbitrator conduct, as seen in the 2018 CPTPP [15]); (3) adding an appeal mechanism (e.g., the hybrid approach in China's proposal at UNCITRAL [3]); or (4) completely replacing the ISDS mechanism with an adjudicative body (e.g., the EU investment court [21]). Notably, although UNCITRAL established Working Group III to focus specifically on ISDS reform, years of work and effort have shown that states still find it difficult to reach a consensus on the fundamental reforms [22].

The ongoing investment treaty reforms—particularly the balancing practice between investment protection and the right of states to regulate—has also significantly impacted China's fourth-generation investment treaties. As discussed in Chap. 3, the post-2008 Chinese investment treaties reflect inconsistent balancing practices. This inherent inconsistency stems from the continuously evolving landscape of the international investment regime. On the other hand, it demonstrates that China's fourth-generation investment treaties could have implications for investment treaty reforms, as will be discussed in Chaps 6 and 7.

### 5.2.3 The Fundamental Reform of China's Foreign Investment Regulatory Regime

As discussed, one of China's key objectives in the China-US BIT negotiations was to advance domestic reforms. Consequently, in 2013 China agreed to adopt the pre-establishment national treatment and negative list approach during the BIT negotiations, while simultaneously establishing Shanghai FTZ as a testing ground for these reforms [23]. Based on these reform efforts, China ultimately achieved substantial liberalization of its foreign investment regulatory regime, as evidenced by the 2019 New Foreign Investment Law [24]. In fact, this foreign investment liberalization constitutes only one part of China's "Reform 2.0" initiative [25, 26].

Specifically, China's Reform 2.0 has been implemented pursuant to the Decision of the Central Committee of the Communist Party of China on Some Major Issues Concerning Comprehensively Deepening the Reform, adopted at the Third Plenary Session of the 18th Central Committee in 2013. As the name suggests, this represents a second wave of domestic reform comparable in significance to the 1978 economic reform [26]. The economic reform naturally constitutes the core of China's Reform 2.0, with the fundamental issue being how to properly balance the roles of government and market [27]. The Decision explicitly affirms that the market should play a decisive role in resource allocation, and the government should minimize market intervention [27].

One may wonder why foreign investment liberalization constitutes only one part of China's "Reform 2.0" initiative. This is because the ultimate goal of "Reform 2.0" is to "provide a unified level playing field for all categories of investors, foreign or domestic and public or private" [26]. The Decision specifically emphasizes that:

> "We will implement a unified market access system; and *on the basis of making a negative list, all kinds of market players may enter areas not on the negative list on an equal basis and according to law.* We will explore a management model for foreign investors with pre-entry national treatment plus a negative list." [27]

This suggests that China not only accepts the pre-establishment national treatment and negative list approach in its investment treaties, but also extends the negative list model to regulate its domestic investment market. Consequently, two distinct types of negative lists exist: one applicable to all investors (general negative list) and the other specifically for foreign investors (specific negative list) [28]:

(1) Regarding the general negative list, China in 2015 promulgated the Opinions on Implementing the Market Access Negative List Regime [28]. According to the Opinions, the general negative list regime was piloted in selected regions from 2015 to 2017 to gain experience, and a unified version was implemented in 2018 [28]. The 2018 general negative list initially contained 151 prohibited and restricted sectors, which were further reduced to 106 by 2025 [29, 30].

(2) As for the specific negative list, as outlined in Chap. 2, China released its 2018 version with 48 special administrative measures [31]. This number was subsequently reduced, with the 2024 version retaining only 29 measures [32]. It

is important to distinguish the specific negative list from those in investment treaties, and the 2015 Opinions explicitly state that treaty-negotiated negative lists should prevail [28].

Behind this comprehensive market access reform is that both foreign investors and domestic private investors have long called for a more open investment market in China. The relationship between the market and the government needs to be rebalanced. This issue was not limited to the Third Plenary Session of the 18th Central Committee in 2013. In fact, it has been a persistent issue throughout China's economic reform process. The "Open Door" policy was adopted in 1978, but China initially maintained that the plan should play the primary role. In 1993, with the establishment of the "socialist market economy", the market's role became "fundamental" [33]. In 2013, the market's decisive role in resource allocation was finally recognized [27].

To conclude, China's foreign investment liberalization and, more broadly, its Reform 2.0 provide the fundamental basis for promoting investment liberalization under the fourth generation of investment treaties. China has gone beyond the pre-establishment national treatment and negative list to address other liberalization provisions, notably absolute market access obligations, SOE disciplines and performance requirement prohibition. It is therefore evident that China's comprehensive treaty commitments on investment liberalization are grounded in its open and liberalized foreign investment regulatory regime.

### *5.2.4 China's Growing OFDI and Evolving Role in International Investment*

Regarding the impact of China's FDI and OFDI on its investment treaty practice, as discussed in Chaps. 1 and 3, China's first- and second-generation investment treaties were concluded from the perspective of a capital importer [1]. At the time, with the adoption of "Open Door" policy, China needed to attract foreign investment for its economic development, and the conclusion of investment treaties served as an international instrument to achieve this objective. Meanwhile, the domestic regulatory regime for foreign investment was established step by step. Through these efforts, China's FDI inflows increased significantly.

When it comes to the third generation of investment treaties, China changed its attitude to investment protection from conservative to liberal, primarily for two reasons: to promote OFDI and to continue attracting FDI. For OFDI development, the Going Global Strategy was first proposed in 1998 and later incorporated into the Tenth Five-Year Plan (2001–2005) [34]. In 2004, approval procedurals for OFDI projects were decentralized and simplified [35, 36]. Regarding FDI, China's policy focus transitioned from quantity to quality in 2006 [37]. This suggests that China begun to give priority for high-quality FDI over large-scale inflow. Domestic FDI laws and regulations were correspondingly revised, such as the elimination of preferential tax treatment for foreign enterprises under the 2007 Enterprise Income Tax Law [37, 38].

Between 2004 and 2010, China's OFDI grew substantially, narrowing the gap with FDI. In 2011, China investment policies had evolved to balance FDI and OFDI. In the Twelfth Five-Year Plan (2011–2015), China emphasized improving the investment environment and safeguarding foreign investors' legal rights for FDI, while enhancing relevant systems and negotiating international agreements for OFDI protection [39]. This evolution demonstrates that as China's OFDI expanded significantly, its attitude toward investment protection changed accordingly, notably beginning to use investment treaties to protect its overseas investments.

In 2013, China adopted the BRI, encouraging Chinese enterprises to participate in investment and development in countries along the BRI. This initiative has significantly stimulated China's OFDI flows. In 2015, the amounts of China's FDI and OFDI amounts reached comparable levels, at 136 and 128 billion of dollars respectively [40]. As noted in Chap. 1, according to UNCTAD, China consistently ranked among the top five economies for both FDI and OFDI between 2022 and 2024 [41–43]. Consequently, it is now widely acknowledged that China has transitioned from being solely a capital importer to becoming both a capital importer and exporter. China's growing OFDI and its evolving role in international law have undoubtedly exerted substantial influence on its fourth-generation investment treaty practice.

### 5.2.5 China's Increasing Involvement in Investment Treaty Arbitration

As noted, 28 investment arbitration cases have been brought under Chinese investment treaties to date, with 20 by Chinese investors and 8 against the Chinese government [44]. Notably, around 60% (18 cases) of these cases were brought in the past five years, with 14 by Chinese investors and 4 against the Chinese government [44]. This trend suggests an increasing number of Chinese investors and foreign investors in China have resorted to the ISDS mechanism to resolve investment disputes.

A closer examination of the 20 cases brought by Chinese investors (9 cases have concluded) reveals that outcomes primarily fall into four categories: (1) Awards in favor of Chinese investors granting compensation, as evidenced in *Tza Yap Shum v. Peru* and *Zhongshan Fucheng v. Nigeria* [45, 46]; (2) Jurisdictional decisions in favor of Chinese investors, followed by settlements with host states as evidenced in *Beijing Urban Construction v. Yemen* and *Wang v. Finland* [47, 48]; (3) Dismissals due to lack of jurisdiction, primarily concerning the interpretation of restrictive ISDS provisions, as evidenced in *Beijing Shougang and others v. Mongolia* [49]; and (4) Successful jurisdiction but dismissal on merits, as evidenced in *Sanum Investments v. Laos* [50]. Overall, Chinese investors face significant challenges in first overcoming jurisdictional hurdles.

As for 8 cases brought against the Chinese government, the key issues have consistently revolved around the interpretation of restrictive ISDS provisions. Notably, China for the first time clarified its official stance on these provisions—advocating for a narrow interpretation—in *AsiaPhos and Norwest v. China*, as extensively analyzed in Chap. 4 [51]. To date, China's experience with investment arbitration has been largely positive, and critically, the government has expressed willingness to actively engage in such proceedings. Given this growing practical experience, it can be expected that China will play a more proactive role in reforming the investment treaty regime.

Beyond the interpretation of restrictive ISDS provisions, many other issues have arisen, including (1) the application of Chinese investment treaties to Hong Kong and Macao SARs; (2) the coverage of SOEs under Chinese investment treaties; and (3) the interpretation of fork-in-the-road provisions. These issues, analyzed in Chaps. 3 and 4, may significantly influence China's future investment treaty practice. Notably, some matters are unique to China (e.g., Hong Kong and Macao application) or particularly crucial for China (e.g., SOE coverage). Consequently, China's increasing involvement in investment arbitration has been substantially shaping its fourth-generation investment treaty practice.

In conclusion, this section has identified five key drivers behind China's fourth-generation investment treaties. As emphasized earlier, these factors are dynamic and continue to evolve. Given that these treaties still face certain challenges—particularly concerning ISDS reform—the development of these five factors will critically determine China's ultimate position on its fourth-generation investment treaty practice.

## 5.3 The Network of Chinese Investment Treaties: Bilateral, Regional and Multilateral Levels

As noted in Chap. 1, to date, China has developed a comprehensive network of investment treaties with 109 BITs and 30 TIPs currently in force [52]. The first issue that arises is whether there is any difference between Chinese BITs and TIPs (mostly referring to FTAs). Generally speaking, FTAs—with their aim to increase FDI flows—typically include BIT-plus obligations, especially concerning market access, performance requirement prohibitions, regulatory transparency, environmental protection and labor rights [12, 53]. As noted in Chap. 2, these liberalization-related issues were initially introduced in the 2004 US Model BIT due to the US objective of reconciling BITs with FTAs [12].

On this issue, Kong undertook a comprehensive comparison between the 2012 China-Canada BIT and the investment chapters of the 2006 China-Pakistan FTA, 2008 China-New Zealand FTA, 2009 China-Peru FTA and 2009 China-ASEAN FTA, concluding that Chinese FTAs do not impose additional investment obligations [53]. However, it should be noted that some liberalization-related issues were first addressed in Chinese FTAs. For example, the 2008 China-New Zealand FTA was the first to emphasized that attracting foreign investment should not be achieved at the expense of lowering labor rights [54]. Additionally, the transparency provisions in the 2015 China-Australia FTA are more comprehensive than those in the 2012 China-Canada BIT [55, 56].

Second, it should be noted that, despite the emergence of the fourth generation of investment treaties, China has tended to adopt a flexible negotiation strategy in practice—often relying on the models of partner countries as a basis for negotiations [57]. Berger argued that China's adaptive strategy could be attributed to its pragmatism in "getting deals done" [57]. Other explanations included the power struggle between different governmental departments in terms of investment policy [57]. Moreover, as Zhao and Timothy argued, the flexible negotiation strategy has also been adopted in Chinese FTAs, including their investment chapters [58, 59]. The following section explores China's investment treaty network across multiple levels—bilateral, regional, and multilateral.

### 5.3.1 Bilateral Level

At the bilateral level, China has concluded BITs and FTAs with its treaty partners. China launched its BIT program in 1982, and following the WTO Doha fallout, it began to conclude FTAs in 2002 [53]. Many of China's first-generation BITs were renegotiated during the 2000s, as evidenced by the 2003 China-Germany BIT [60]. These renegotiated Chinese BITs adopted a liberal approach, constituting the third generation of investment treaties. As mentioned in Chap. 3, nearly half of China's existing BITs were concluded under the second-generation framework. It is thus foreseeable that many Chinese BITs will be terminated and potentially renegotiated in the future. China's new fourth-generation investment treaty practice will likely exert influence on this process.

In addition, China has engaged in BIT negotiations with two key partners: the US and the EU. The China-US and China-EU BIT negotiations have significantly shaped the development of China's fourth-generation investment treaties—particularly regarding investment liberalization—as extensively discussed in Chap. 2. It is noteworthy that the China-US BIT negotiations were suspended after the Trump Administration took office in 2017. Notably, the US later shifted its BIT approach, as evidenced by the 2018 USMCA which introduced a selective application of ISDS provisions [20]. Whether this reflects the US final position remains uncertain. In contrast, China and the EU reached an agreement in principle on CAI in 2020 [13]. As previously detailed, the 2020 CAI has prompted China to make extensive commitments to investment liberalization, playing a significant role in shaping the fourth generation of Chinese investment treaties.

Moreover, China has been advised to renegotiate BITs with countries along the BRI. According to recent research conducted by Bath, China has already concluded BITs with most BRI countries, but most of these treaties were signed during 1980s and 1990s, when China adopted a conservative approach to investment treaties—particularly by incorporating restrictive ISDS provisions [61]. Consequently, China's existing BITs with BRI countries may fail to provide adequate protection for its OFDI projects. Therefore, it would be necessary to renegotiate these treaties with BRI countries [61]. Additionally, some scholars suggested that enhanced investment protection might also be achieved through China's accession to the Energy Charter Treaty (ECT), as most "Belt" countries are already the ECT members while many "Road" countries are potential members due to the ongoing modernization of the Energy Charter framework [62].

### 5.3.2 *Regional Level*

At the regional level, China concluded an investment agreement with ASEAN in 2009 [63]. Furthermore, China, Japan and Korea concluded an investment treaty in 2012 [64]. More significantly, China finalized the RCEP in 2020, with includes the ASEAN, Japan, Korea, Australia and New Zealand [16]. As discussed in Chap. 3, the 2020 RCEP has played a significant role in shaping China's fourth-generation investment treaties by prompting to further refine substantive protection provisions in line with contemporary trends in investment treaty practice.

In the Pacific Rim region, another mega-regional trade agreement exists—the 2018 CPTPP [15]. In 2021, China formally applied to join the CPTPP. In June 2025, China announced that, following its application, it had conducted in-depth analysis, evaluation and preparatory work, and was already "fully prepared to join" the CPTPP [65]. China also reaffirmed its commitment to "align actively with high-standard international economic and trade rules such as those of the CPTPP, expand its institutional openness steadily, and continue undertaking in-depth communication and exchanges with all members" [65]. It remains to be seen whether and when China will join the CPTPP. However, undoubtedly, accession to the CPTPP would significantly advance the development of China's fourth-generation investment treaties.

### 5.3.3 *Multilateral Level*

Historically, numerous efforts were undertaken to create a comprehensive multilateral investment treaty, yet none ultimately succeeded. The most significant one was the OECD Multilateral Agreement on Investment (MAI) initiative during the 1990s, in which China participated as an observer [66]. Despite these failures, a multilateral treaty does exist in the energy sector—the ECT signed in 1994 [67]. The ECT currently has 53 signatories, and its scope extends beyond investment protection to include energy trade, cross-border energy transit flows, and energy efficiency [68]. The ECT has been expanding its geographical coverage to promote global energy cooperation, with the International Energy Charter (IEC) adopted as a political declaration in 2015 [69, 70].

China became an observer of the ECT in 2001 and signed the IEC in 2015 [62]. In the past decades, China's investment treaties have undergone significant generational changes, as discussed earlier. In recent years, Chinese scholars have discussed whether China should accede to the ECT. On the one hand, recent Chinese investment treaty practice is seen as "almost compatible with the ECT practice" [62, 71]. On the other hand, concerns remain that the Chinese government could face investment arbitration claims due to ongoing energy policy reforms [72]. Nevertheless, both sides agree that ECT accession would bring significant benefits to China, including enhanced protection for China's OFDI in BRI countries [62, 71, 72, 73].

In December 2024, the Energy Charter Conference adopted and approved four modernization decisions for the ECT, including treaty amendments [74]. The amendments clarified several key provisions, such as the FET and FPS standards as well as indirect expropriation, while also optimizing arbitral proceedings [75]. These changes partially align with the balancing approach seen in China's fourth-generation investment treaties. Yet, whether China will engage further with the ECT remains to be seen.

## 5.4 Conclusion

As demonstrated, the fourth generation of Chinese investment treaties have emerged, characterized by a liberal approach to investment liberalization and a balanced approach to investment protection. The emergence of the fourth generation of Chinese investment treaties can be mainly attributed to five major factors: (1) the changing landscape of investment treaties; (2) the need to balance investment protection with the right of states to regulate; (3) the fundamental reform of China's foreign investment regulatory regime; (4) China's growing ODFI and evolving role in international law; and (5) China's increasing involvement in international arbitration. So far, through these four generations of treaties, China has established a comprehensive investment treaty network at the bilateral, regional and multilateral levels.

## References

1. Norah Gallagher and Wenhua Shan (2009) Chinese Investment Treaties: Policies and Practice. Oxford
2. UNCTAD (2020) International Investment Agreements Reform Accelerator. Switzerland
3. UNCITRAL (2019) A/CN.9/WG.III/WP.177 Possible Reform of Investor-State Dispute Settlement (ISDS): Submission from the Government of China. https://docs.un.org/en/A/CN.9/WG.III/WP.177. Accessed 12 August 2025

4. Anthea Roberts and Taylor St John (2019) UNCITRAL and ISDS Reform: China's Proposal. Blog of the European Journal of International Law. https://www.ejiltalk.org/uncitral-and-isds-reform-chinas-proposal/. Accessed 12 August 2025
5. UNCTAD (2015) World Investment Report 2015: Reforming International Investment Governance. Switzerland
6. Germany-Pakistan BIT (1959)
7. Chinese Model BIT Version I (1984)
8. Chinese Model BIT Version II (1989)
9. Chinese Model BIT Version III (1997)
10. UNCTAD (2017) World Investment Report 2017: Investment and The Digital Economy. Switzerland
11. European Commission, Investment-the pillars. https://trade.ec.europa.eu/access-to-markets/en/content/investment-pillars. Accessed 7 August 2025
12. Kenneth. J. Vandevelde (2009) A Comparison of the 2004 and 1994 U.S. Model BITs: Rebalancing Investor and Host Country Interests. In: Karl. P. Sauvant (ed), Yearbook on International Investment Law & Policy 2008–2009. Oxford, pp. 283–316
13. China-EU Comprehensive Agreement on Investment (2020)
14. European Commission, Investment. https://policy.trade.ec.europa.eu/help-exporters-and-importers/accessing-markets/investment_en. Accessed 7 August 2025
15. Comprehensive and Progressive Agreement for Trans-Pacific Partnership (2018)
16. Regional Comprehensive Economic Partnership (2020)
17. The WTO Investment Facilitation for Development Agreement (2024)
18. WTO, The Investment Facilitation for Development (IFD) Agreement. https://www.wto.org/english/tratop_e/invfac_public_e/invfac_intro_e.htm. Accessed 7 August 2025
19. Chin Leng Lim (2020) Reaching for Utopia, Geneva as Inspiration for Investment Disputes? In: Meredith Kolsky Lewis, Junji Nakagawa, Rostam J. Neuwirth, Colin B. Picker, and Peter-Tobias Stoll (ed) A Post-WTO International Legal Order Utopian, Dystopian and Other Scenarios. Springer, Switzerland, pp. 167–185
20. United States-Mexico-Canada Agreement (2018)
21. European Commission, Guide to Investment Court System. https://webgate.acceptance.ec.europa.eu/portal9/en/content/guide-investment-court-system. Accessed 11 August 2025
22. Anthea Roberts and Taylor St John (2023) UNCITRAL and ISDS Reform: Moving to the Delivery Phase. Blog of the European Journal of International Law. https://www.ejiltalk.org/uncitral-and-isds-reform-moving-to-the-delivery-phase/. Accessed 11 August 2025
23. U.S. Department of the Treasury (2013) Joint U.S.-China Economic Track Fact Sheet of the Fifth Meeting of the U.S.-China Strategic and Economic Dialogue. https://home.treasury.gov/news/press-releases/jl2010 Accessed 7 August 2025
24. Foreign Investment Law of the People's Republic of China (2019)
25. Jingjie Yang (2013) Reform 2.0 to be Unveiled. Global Times. https://www.globaltimes.cn/content/823892.shtml. Accessed 7 August 2025
26. Wenhua Shan and Hongrui Chen (2016) China-US BIT Negotiation and the Emerging Chinese BIT 4.0. In: C. L. Lim (ed), Alternative Visions of the International Law on Foreign Investment: Essays in Honour of Muthucumaraswamy Sornarajah. Cambridge, pp. 223–254
27. Decision of the Central Committee of the Communist Party of China on Some Major Issues Concerning Comprehensively Deepening the Reform (2013)
28. Opinions of the State Council on Implementing the Market Access Negative List Regime (2015)
29. Notice by the National Development and Reform Commission and the Ministry of Commerce of Issuance of the Market Access Negative List (2018)
30. Notice by the National Development and Reform Commission, the Ministry of Commerce, and the State Administration for Market Regulation of Issuance of the Market Access Negative List (2025)
31. Special Administrative Measures (Negative List) for the Access of Foreign Investment (2018)
32. Special Administrative Measures (Negative List) for the Access of Foreign Investment (2024)

33. Decision of the of the Central Committee of the Communist Party of China on Some Issues Concerning the Establishment of a Socialist Market Economic (1993)
34. Outline of the 10th Five-Year Plan (2001–2005) for the National Economic and Social Development of the People's Republic of China (2001)
35. Interim Measures for the Administration of Examination and Approval of the Overseas Investment Projects (2004)
36. Provisions on the Examination and Approval of Investment to Run Enterprises Abroad (2004)
37. Wenhua Shan, Norah Gallagher and Sheng Zhang (2012) National Treatment for Foreign Investment in China: A Changing Landscape. ICSID Review, Volume 27, Issue 1: 120–144
38. Enterprise Income Tax Law of the People's Republic of China (2007)
39. Outline of the 12th Five-Year Plan (2011–2015) for the National Economic and Social Development of the People's Republic of China (2011)
40. UNCTAD (2016) World Investment Report 2016: Investor Nationality: Policy Challenges. Switzerland
41. UNCTAD (2023) World Investment Report 2023: Investing in Sustainable Energy for All. Switzerland
42. UNCTAD (2024) World Investment Report 2024: Investment Facilitation and Digital Government. Switzerland
43. UNCTAD (2025) World Investment Report 2025: International Investment in the Digital Economy. Switzerland
44. UNCTAD, China-Investment Dispute Settlement Navigator. https://investmentpolicy.unctad.org/investment-dispute-settlement/country/42/china/investor. Accessed 15 August 2025
45. Señor Tza Yap Shum v. The Republic of Peru, ICSID Case No. ARB/07/6
46. Zhongshan Fucheng Industrial Investment Co. Ltd. v. Federal Republic of Nigeria (ad hoc)
47. Beijing Urban Construction Group Co. Ltd. v. Republic of Yemen, ICSID Case No. ARB/14/30
48. Wang Jiazhu v. Republic of Finland (2013 UNCITRAL Arbitration Rules)
49. Beijing Shougang and others v. Mongolia, PCA Case No. 2010-20
50. Sanum Investments v. Lao People's Democratic Republic, PCA Case No. 2013–13, Award on Jurisdiction (13 December 2013)
51. AsiaPhos Limited and Norwest Chemicals Pte Ltd v. People's Republic of China, ICSID Case No. ADM/21/1
52. UNCTAD, China- International Investment Agreements Navigator. https://investmentpolicy.unctad.org/international-investment-agreements/countries/42/china. Accessed 15 August 2025
53. Qingjiang Kong (2013) Bilateral Investment Rule-Making: BITs or FTAs with Investment Rules? Journal of World Investment & Trade, Volume 14, Issue 4: 638-645
54. China-New Zealand FTA, Memorandum of Understanding on Labor Cooperation (2008)
55. China-Australia FTA (2015)
56. China-Canada BIT (2012)
57. Axel Berger (2015) Hesitant Embrace: China's Recent Approach to International Investment Rule-Making. Journal of World Investment & Trade, Volume 16: 843–868
58. Jun Zhao and Webster Timothy (2011) Taking Stock: China's First Decade of Free Trade. University of Pennsylvania Journal of International Law, Volume 33, Issue 1: 65–119
59. Heng Wang (2017) The RCEP and Its Investment Rules: Learning from Past Chinese FTAs. The Chinese Journal of Global Governance, Volume 3, Issue 2: 160–181
60. China-Germany BIT (2003)
61. Vivienne Bath (2016) "One Belt, One Road" and China's Outbound Investment Regime. In: Lutz-Christian Wolff and Chao Xi (ed) Legal Dimensions of China's Belt and Road Initiative. Kluwer, Hong Kong, pp. 139–164
62. Wenhua Shan (2015) Report on the Compatibility of Chinese Laws and Regulations with the Energy Charter Treaty. Brussels
63. China-ASEAN Investment Agreement (2009)
64. China-Japan-Korea Trilateral Investment Agreement (2012)

65. China's Ministry of Commerce (2025) China Fully Prepared to Join CPTPP: Commerce Ministry. https://english.mofcom.gov.cn/News/SignificantNews/art/2025/art_77c3e39567064529b82ab8f5b1a7db33.html. Accessed 15 August 2025
66. UNCTAD (1999) Lessons From the MAI. https://unctad.org/system/files/official-document/psiteiitm22.en.pdf. Accessed 15 August 2025
67. Energy Charter Treaty (1994)
68. Energy Charter, The Energy Charter Treaty. https://www.energycharter.org/process/energy-charter-treaty-1994/energy-charter-treaty/. Accessed 15 August 2025
69. Energy Charter, The International Energy Charter, https://www.energycharter.org/process/international-energy-charter-2015/overview/. Accessed 15 August 2025
70. Energy Charter (2010) Road Map for the Modernisation of the Energy Charter Process, https://www.energycharter.org/fileadmin/DocumentsMedia/News/20101124-Energy_Charter_Process_Modernisation_Road_Map.pdf. Accessed 15 August 2025
71. Sheng Zhang (2012) The Energy Charter Treaty and China: Member or Bystander? Journal of World Investment & Trade Volume 13, Issue 4: 597–617
72. Libin Zhang (2016) Risks for Chinese Investors in the One Belt One Road Initiative. Asia law. https://www.asialaw.com/NewsAndAnalysis/risks-for-chinese-investors-in-the-one-belt-one-road-initiative/Index/85. Accessed 15 August 2025
73. Steivan Defilla (2015) Energy Charter's Modernisation in the Future. https://www.energycharter.org/fileadmin/DocumentsMedia/IAP/20150721/IAP20150721-SO-SDefilla.pdf. Accessed 15 August 2025
74. Energy Charter (2024) The Energy Charter Conference Adopts Decisions on the Modernisation of the Energy Charter Treaty. https://www.energycharter.org/media/news/article/the-energy-charter-conference-adopts-decisions-on-the-modernisation-of-the-energy-charter-treaty/. Accessed 15 August 2025
75. Amendments to the Energy Charter Treaty (2024)

# Chapter 6
# The Global Backlash Against Investment Arbitration and Investment Treaty Reform

Chapters 2 through 5 analyze the key features of and driving factors behind China's fourth-generation investment treaties, while this chapter and Chap. 7 evaluate their broader implications for international investment law. To this end, this chapter first outlines recent trends and developments in international investment law, covering both the global backlash against investment arbitration (Sect. 6.1) and the subsequent reforms to the investment treaty regime (Sect. 6.2). Notably, these reforms have been undertaken not only at the national level but also at the bilateral, regional, and multilateral levels. Against this backdrop, the chapter concludes with a comprehensive assessment of the ongoing investment treaty reforms (Sect. 6.3).

## 6.1 Global Backlash Against Investment Arbitration

As discussed, the international investment regime has undergone a "legitimacy crisis" over the past two decades [1]. This crisis has been largely driven by arbitral tribunals adopting expansive interpretations of treaty standards. A key example is the broad reading of the FET standard. In *Tecmed v. Mexico*, the tribunal incorporated investor expectations into the FET standard, justifying it by the treaty preamble's promotion objective [2, 3]. Similarly, in *Occidental v. Ecuador*, the tribunal interpreted FET to guarantee a stable legal environment, a finding that also underpinned a breach of the FPS obligation [4]. These rulings demonstrate how tribunals have elevated the treaty standards, thereby granting more protection to foreign investors.

The expansive interpretations also occurred in NAFTA ISDS cases. Three NAFTA member states felt that these expansive interpretations did not align with their original intent [5]. As a result, on 31 July 2001, the FTC issued an Interpretation Note reaffirming that international law referred solely to customary international law, and that the FET and FPS standards provided protection no greater than the customary minimum standard of treatment [6]. This reaffirmation was a response to awards like



J. Chao, *The Emerging Fourth Generation of Chinese Investment Treaties*,
https://doi.org/10.1007/978-981-95-5052-4_6

*Pope & Talbot v. Canada,* where the tribunal held that NAFTA investors were entitled to customary minimum standard of treatment plus fairness [5, 7].

In addition, the FTC's Note clarified that a breach of other NAFTA provisions did not automatically constitute a violation of the FET and FPS standards [6]. This Note also required the timely publication of case documents to enhance arbitral transparency, a concern highlighted in a New York Times report [6, 8].

The NAFTA backlash led to the reformulation of investment treaties among its member states. In 2004, both the US and Canada released updated versions of their Model BITs. The minimum standard of treatment provisions incorporated the FTC's Interpretation Note, while arbitral transparency was significantly enhanced [9, 10]. That same year, the tribunal in *Methanex v. US* ruled that a non-discriminatory regulatory measure for a legitimate public policy objective did not constitute expropriation [5, 11]. This ruling was incorporated in the 2004 US Model BIT as an expropriation exception [9].

Regarding the expansive interpretations in arbitral awards, Sornarajah argued that these developments were driven by "neoliberalism" [12]. Following the collapse of the Soviet Union in the early 1990s, the "Washington Consensus" emerged as the dominant mode of governance, with neoliberalism shaping the regulation of economic activities as well as the rules of international trade and investment [12]. Consequently, investment protection undoubtedly became the crucial purpose of investment treaties [13]. Similarly, Alvarez observed that the current backlash against investment arbitration in state practice, including the recalibration of the US Model BIT, signaled a growing loss of confidence in the "Washington Consensus" and its neoliberal strategies [14].

The recalibration of Model BITs failed to alleviate ISDS criticisms. On the contrary, these criticisms intensified and expanded to encompass both substantive and procedural concerns. Substantively, critics argued that arbitral tribunals continued to interpret investment treaties expansively [15] and that the system exhibited systemic bias in favor of foreign investors [16, 17]. Procedurally, criticisms primarily focused on the inconsistency of arbitral awards, conflicting interests of arbitrators, high cost of investment arbitration, and discrimination caused against domestic investors [16, 18]. More significantly, many scholars and policymakers questioned whether the current international investment regime unduly constrained host states' regulatory power [12, 17].

The growing criticisms of investment arbitration triggered a global backlash. In 2007, Bolivia denounced the ICSID Convention, followed by Ecuador and Venezuela in 2010 and 2012 respectively [19, 20, 21]. These withdrawals gave rise to complex legal uncertainties, particularly regarding their implications for pending claims as well as the constitutional issues on ICSID and BITs [22, 23]. In 2010, South Africa decided to terminate its existing investment treaties and no longer conclude new ones in the future, and subsequently in 2015 required domestic mediation be used for investor-state dispute resolution [24, 25]. Similarly, in 2014, Indonesia decided to terminate its investment treaties. Many attributed Indonesia's decision to the *Churchill Mining v. Indonesia* case, but others argued that it resulted from a combination of factors, such as the rise of economic nationalism in Indonesia [26]. It was reported that Indonesia would consider renegotiating investment treaties based on a modern template [27].

Surprisingly, in 2011, Australia announced a new trade policy stating that ISDS provisions would no longer be included in its future investment treaties [28]. The Gillard government justified this decision by arguing that, in light of national treatment, foreign investors should not enjoy greater legal rights than domestic investors [28]. This rationale appeared questionable, as investment arbitration has been established for decades [29]. The policy shift likely stemmed from the *Philip Morris v. Australia* case, in which Australia's Tobacco Plain Packaging Act—a public health measure banning the display of graphic symbols on tobacco products—was challenged [28, 30].

More significantly, Australia soon reversed its position on ISDS provisions. In 2013, the Abbott government announced that it would evaluate including ISDS provisions in future investment treaties on a case-by-case basis [31]. This shift led to the incorporation of comprehensive ISDS mechanisms in both the 2014 Australia-Korea FTA and 2015 Australia-China FTA [32, 33]. This case-by-case approach drew criticism, prompting calls for a more transparent framework. In June 2015, Australia's Senate Foreign Affairs called for the creation of a model treaty for future negotiations, stipulating that it should include the ISDS mechanism [34]. Reversing course again, Australia declared in 2022 that it would exclude the ISDS mechanism from all new treaties for the right of states to regulate [35]. Consistent with this policy, the 2024 Australia-United Arab Emirates Agreement omits ISDS provisions entirely [36].

Amid this global backlash, except for these radical actions, most countries—including the US, the EU, China and India—have reformulated their investment treaties. According to UNCTAD, at least fifty countries have been updating their Model BITs, with most seeking to balance investment protection with the right of states to regulate [37]. These balancing practices reflect their evolving investment policy priorities.

## 6.2 Investment Treaty Reform

In response to growing criticisms of investment arbitration, treaty reform has emerged at the multiple levels: national (through revised Model BITs), bilateral, regional, and multilateral [37]. At the national level, the US, the EU and India serve as prominent examples of this reform trend, whose approaches will be examined in detail in this section.

## 6.2.1 National Level

### 6.2.1.1 US Model

As previously discussed, the 2004 US Model BIT emerged largely in response to the NAFTA backlash. Additional factors, as Vandevelde noted, included the US desire to reconcile BITs with FTAs and align with the negotiating objectives established under the Bipartisan Trade Promotion Authority Act: reducing investment barriers while guaranteeing foreign investors receive treatment no more favorable than US domestic investors [5, 38].

Specifically, a significant objective of the 2004 US Model BIT was to strengthen state control over arbitral tribunals through substantive and procedural reforms [5]. Substantively, the minimum standard of treatment provision incorporated the FTC's Interpretation Note while indirect expropriation was clarified through its definition, determination and exception [5, 9]. These clarifications, as discussed in Chap. 3, have significantly influenced investment treaty practices in some other countries, including the EU and China. Procedurally, to enhance the efficiency of ISDS mechanism, the 2004 US Model BIT introduced new provisions addressing claim consolidation and arbitral transparency [5, 9]. Furthermore, contracting states were authorized to issue joint decisions on treaty interpretation, which would be binding on tribunals [5, 9].

Another significant objective was to preserve more regulatory space for host states mainly through incorporating exception clauses [5]. The 1994 US Model BIT contained three general exception clauses addressing a state's national security, peace obligations, and special formalities [39].The 2004 US Model BIT expanded these exceptions to encompass a state's right to regulate financial services and maintain the confidentiality of information and so forth [9]. Furthermore, as previously discussed, it introduced an expropriation exception for non-discriminatory measures adopted for legitimate public policy objectives [9].

Overall, the 2004 US Model BIT sought to balance the interests and obligations of foreign investors and host states [5]. Alvarez characterized the 2004 US Model BIT as "recalibration" [14]. He argued that the 1984–1987 "golden age" of US BITs—marked by strong investment protection standards—had passed, and the US begun to emphasize the role of host states as regulators of foreign investment [40].

In 2009, following the President Obama's election and the financial crisis, the US government commenced another review of the US Model BIT [41]. The review focused primarily on three issues: the ISDS mechanism, SOE disciplines and financial service regulation [41]. Although this review sparked public debate and generated numerous reform proposals, the 2012 US Model BIT retained most of the substantive and procedural provisions from previous versions [41]. As demonstrated below, the 2012 US Model BIT did not resolve investment arbitration criticisms, ultimately leading to the selective adoption of the ISDS mechanism in the 2018 USMCA.

#### 6.2.1.2 EU Model

European countries have long been active players in the field of investment treaty making. With the entry into force of the Treaty of Lisbon in 2009, the EU gained competence to conclude investment agreements on behalf of its member states [42, 43]. In 2010, the EU issued a comprehensive international investment policy, emphasizing that both investment protection and liberalization were key instruments for its strategy [44]. To date, the EU has concluded investment agreements with Canada, Singapore, Vietnam and Chile, while agreement negotiations are ongoing with countries such as China, India, Indonesia, Malaysia, and the Philippines [45].

Notably, the EU negotiated an FTA with the US between 2013 and 2016—the Transatlantic Trade and Investment Partnership (TTIP). During the negotiations, the ISDS mechanism sparked public concern across the EU, with some NGOs denouncing its provisions as "a threat to democracy" [46]. In response, the EU in 2014 launched a public consultation on TTIP's substantive and procedural provisions [47, 48]. In 2015, the EU adopted a new investment policy for TTIP negotiations and future BITs/FTAs. The new policy concentrated on two key elements: (1) establishing an investment court to replace the ISDS mechanism; and (2) clarifying protection clauses to strike a balance between foreign investors and host states [49, 50]

For the first element, the EU proposed a multilateral investment court project in 2016. According to the EU, the multilateral investment court would (1) comprise a first-instance tribunal and an appellate tribunal; (2) operate as a permanent institution with transparent procedures; (3) resolve disputes arising out of the existing and future investment treaties; (4) provide an effective enforcement mechanism; and (5) be open to accession by all interested countries [51]. As examined in Chap. 4, this investment court model was subsequently incorporated into the 2016 CETA, with the EU and Canada establishing comprehensive operational rules for its implementation [52].

For the second element, a significant innovation involved adopting a closed-list approach to define the FET and FPS standards, as discussed in Chap. 3. This closed-list approach reflects the EU's deliberate effort to clarify the scope of the FET and FPS standards and strengthen its control over arbitral tribunals. Furthermore, the EU has consistently underscored the right of states to regulate, as clearly evidenced by the 2016 CETA [52]. As Sornarajah observed, these reforms introduced a competing framework into investment treaties, challenging the neoliberal investment protection model [12].

Today, the EU has expanded its international investment policy to encompass three pillars: investment protection, liberalization and facilitation. Furthermore, the EU has outlined five key objectives: (1) ensuring a level playing field for EU investors; (2) creating a predictable and transparent investment environment; (3) promoting investment for sustainable development; (4) attracting foreign investment, while protecting its own essential interests; and (5) preserving the right of states to regulate in the public interests [53]. These developments have shaped the EU's investment agreements, including the one with China. As examined in Chap. 2, the 2020 CAI has led China to undertake comprehensive and substantial commitments on investment liberalization.

#### 6.2.1.3 Indian Model

In December 2015, India approved its new Model BIT after a nine-month public consultation [54]. The 2015 Indian Model BIT, once released, attracted significant attention from academics and practitioners. In fact, as early as 2013, India decided to suspend all ongoing investment agreement negotiations and to review its existing investment agreements [55]. This decision was largely triggered by the *White Industries v. India* case, the first investment arbitration claim brought against the Indian government [56]. More notably, immediately after this case, seventeen additional investment arbitration notices were issued against India [57].

The 2015 Indian Model BIT seeks to strike a balance between investment protection and the right of states to regulate, as exemplified by its preamble [54]. However, India appears to have taken a more significant step toward tilting the balance toward host states, as evidenced by more restrictive definitions of investment and investor along with the outright removal of the MFN clause [54]. Regarding investment treatment, the 2015 Indian Model BIT also adopts a closed-list approach for the FET and FPS standards, but it goes a step further than the EU by narrowing the scope of these standards even more [54].

Regarding the ISDS mechanism, the 2015 Indian Model BIT imposes stringent conditions. First, arbitral tribunals are explicitly barred from reviewing the decisions of domestic courts [54]. Second, foreign investors are required to exhaust local remedies for at least five years before submitting the disputes to arbitration [54]. This rule prolongs the timeline for investors to access to ISDS. However, Hanessian and Duggal argued that, given the slow pace of India's judiciary, a five-year exhaustion period might be a reasonable compromise [57].

The 2015 Indian Model BIT also includes several distinctive provisions. For example, it considers establishing an appeal body to enhance the coherence of treaty interpretations [54]. It further specifies the key considerations for establishing such a body, including its nature, composition, review scope, and transparency [54]. Furthermore, it enhances foreign investors' obligation and social responsibility by requiring that they comply with domestic laws and regulations, combat corruption, and pay taxes [54].

The 2015 Indian Model BIT expresses discontent with the current international investment regime and advocates for reform. Unsurprisingly, it is often compared with China's recent treaty practice, as both are major emerging economies. For instance, Hanessian and Duggal expressed disappointment with India's approach, arguing that, given India's global economic influence its Model BIT could have contributed meaningfully to the balancing debate between investor protection and state sovereignty [57]. Instead, the 2015 text tilts the balance too far toward host states [57].

Overall, an international consensus has emerged that investment protection should be balanced against the right of states to regulate. However, as the US, EU, Indian Models demonstrate, states have struck this balance differently. As UNCTAD noted, the question of how to achieve an appropriate balance is determined by a state's specific situation, preferences and policies [37]. Nonetheless, achieving consensus in bilateral and/or regional treaty negotiations could mitigate fragmentation and address the global backlash against investment arbitration.

### 6.2.2 Bilateral and Regional Level

Over the past two decades, investment treaty making has seen a shift from bilateral to regional agreements. As identified by UNCTAD, despite the potential for overlaps and inconsistencies, bilateral and regional agreements serve as a crucial platform for promoting treaty reform and rule harmonization [16, 37]. This is particularly evident in two mega-regional agreements: the 2018 CPTPP and the 2020 RCEP.

The CPTPP, also known as the TPP-11, originated from the Trans-Pacific Strategic Economic Partnership Agreements. With the US joining in 2008, the TPP extended to contain twelve members for creating a "twenty-first century trade agreement" [58]. After eight years of negotiations, the TPP was signed in 2016 [59]. However, following the President Trump's election in 2017, the US withdrew. The remaining eleven TPP member states renegotiated and signed the CPTPP on 8 March 2018, incorporating the TPP agreement while suspending certain provisions [60].

The RCEP, launched in 2012, was negotiated among the ASEAN, China, Japan, Korea, Australia, New Zealand and India, building on existing their ASEAN + 1 FTAs to strengthen regional integration. India withdrew in 2019, and the agreement was subsequently finalized in 2020. Notably, the RCEP investment chapter defers ISDS provisions to future negotiations, likely due to growing criticisms of the ISDS mechanism and divergent views among member states regarding its reform [61]. However, foreign investors may still rely on the ISDS provisions in the existing ASEAN + 1 FTAs to protect their investments.

When discussing the potential consolidation of regional investment agreements, attention needs to be paid to their overlaps and inconsistencies [37]. For example, China and Korea have concluded at least four investment agreements in recent years: the 2007 China-Korea BIT, 2012 China-Korea-Japan TIT, 2015 China-Korea FTA, and 2020 RCEP [61–64]. Given these overlaps, conflict clauses may be adopted to address the inconsistencies between these treaties [65]. According to UNCTAD, enhancing coherence between investment treaties represents the third or final phase of investment treaty reform [66].

### 6.2.3 Multilateral Level

So far, the multilateral reform efforts have primarily focused on procedural aspects, as seen in UNCITRAL and ICSID. As discussed in Chap. 4, UNCITRAL Transparency Rules were adopted in 2014 to address public concerns regarding arbitral transparency [67]. Specifically, these rules stipulate that arbitration notices, pleadings, written submissions, hearings, as well as awards should be made available to the public, while persevering the right of parties to maintain confidential or protected information [67]. These rules have also been incorporated in recent investment treaties, as exemplified by the 2016 CETA [52].

In 2017, UNCITRAL established Working Group III to focus specifically on the ISDS reform. By 2022, it was found that states held divergent views on what reforms were viable and even on what Working Group III needed to achieve to meet its mandate [68]. Considering this, Working Group III adopted a plural approach, developing multiple reform proposals and allowing states to selectively participate in preferred proposals [68]. In 2023, as the working process accelerated, the reform process gained momentum and saw the finalization of several key documents concerning mediation and arbitrator conduct [69]. In 2024, Working Group III concluded its work on the ISDS advisory center [70].

More significantly, in April 2024, Working Group III proposed a two-tier standing mechanism comprising Dispute Tribunal and Appeals Tribunal [71]. In October 2024, an intersessional meeting was held in Chengdu of China to discuss the key issues of the appellate mechanism [72]. Based on these efforts, in June 2025, Working Group III revised the draft on the structure and design of the standing mechanism for deliberation at its upcoming 52nd session (September 2025) [73]. Although the prospects for states establishing a consensus on an appellate mechanism are still uncertain, this initiative is undoubtedly exciting and may become a breakthrough for the ISDS reform.

ICSID embarked on the modernization of its rules and regulations in 2016. In August 2018, ICSID published a comprehensive set of amendment proposals after conducting external consultations and internal deliberations [74]. Later, in September 2018, these proposals were discussed among ICSID member states. By integrating lessons from past cases, these amendments aims to promote a more efficient, fair, and balanced arbitration process [75]. In 2022, the amended ICSID rules were approved, introducing enhancements such as greater arbitral transparency, expedited proceedings, regulation of third-party funding, and expanded access to ICSID, among others [76].

The primary focus of multilateral reform efforts on procedural aspects can be attributed to the nature of the existing international investment regime. To date, no multilateral investment framework has been established for foreign investment. Despite several historical attempts—including the Havana Charter in 1948 and the OECD MAI in 1990s—all have ultimately failed [16, 77, 78]. The existing international investment regime is often characterized as a complex patchwork of more than 3000 overlapping agreements [79].

However, the multilateral procedural reforms are widely regarded as insufficient. Consequently, many scholars have called for a new round of multilateral investment agreement negotiations, arguing that the context for such negotiations has changed for two primary reasons [16, 79, 80]. First, the FDI landscape and national interests have evolved significantly: emerging economies have accumulated substantial OFDI and consequently begun to emphasize investment protection, while developed countries—having frequently served as respondents in investment arbitrations—have increasingly considered their interests as capital importers [16, 79, 80]. Second, a large number of investment treaties could provide a foundation for a multilateral framework [79]. While inconsistencies persist between these treaties, these actually underscore the need for a multilateral investment agreement [79].

Scholars have proposed that WTO is a suitable platform for this initiative, given the interrelation between trade and investment [79, 80]. While the Doha Round has long lasted, the recently concluded IFD Agreement demonstrates that the WTO is able to achieve concrete outcomes [81]. Other proposed forums include the G20, OECD, and UNCTAD [16, 79, 80]. As shown below, the OECD has worked on reforming substantive provisions since 2021.

## 6.3 Continued Reform Progress

It should be borne in mind that the global backlash against investment arbitration and the subsequent reforms to investment treaty regime discussed above are not over but still ongoing. For example, the EU has been promoting the investment court, which Canada, Vietnam and Singapore have agreed to adopt, as reflected in their respective investment agreements [52, 82, 83]. The investment court is also one of the key issues in the EU-China BIT negotiations. As discussed in Chap. 4, the EU aims to establish a Multilateral Investment Court replacing the existing ad hoc ISDS mechanism.

Furthermore, the US, Canada and Mexico renegotiated NAFTA and concluded the USMCA in 2018. Surprisingly, the ISDS provisions under USMCA apply only to Mexico-US investment disputes [84]. In other words, Canada-US investment disputes are no longer subject to ISDS, while Canada-Mexico investment disputes need to rely on the 2018 CPTPP [60]. Furthermore, USMCA imposes significant limitations on ISDS provisions. For example, foreign investors may only challenge breaches of national treatment, MFN treatment, or direct expropriation (excluding indirect expropriation) [84]. Additionally, foreign investors are required to turn to domestic courts or administrative tribunals before submitting the claims to arbitration [84]. The US negotiation objective for the USMCA was to ensure that its investors abroad were granted protections consistent with US practice, while stipulating that foreign investors in the US would be afforded rights no greater than those given to domestic investors [85]. Similar language appeared in the 2002 Bipartisan Trade Promotion Authority and shaped the 2004 and 2012 US Model BITs [5]. It remains unclear whether the USMCA reflects a broader shift in US investment policy.

It is also worth noting that Brazil, after decades of silence, has begun to conclude investment agreements with other countries, as exemplified by its 2015 Cooperation and Facilitation Investment Agreement Model [86, 87]. Unlike traditional investment treaties, Brazil's Model emphasizes investment facilitation and cooperation, as highlighted by its title. The preamble reaffirms its dual aim: to establish a favorable investment environment while safeguarding the regulatory space of host states [86].

It retains traditional investment provisions, such as national treatment, MFN treatment and expropriation, but excludes FET and FPS standards [86]. Additionally, it establishes dispute prevention mechanisms [86].

More significantly, UNCITRAL and OECD have been working on procedural and substantive reforms respectively. As previously discussed, UNCITRAL Working Group III has achieved some outcomes in terms of individual reforms, such as promoting mediation, regulating arbitrator conduct and establishing advisory center, and is aiming for a more ambitious initiative—creating a standing mechanism with an appellate mechanism. Whether it succeeds or fails, Working Group III provides a platform for states to discuss the ISDS reform collectively. In contrast, the OECD begun its reform efforts in 2021. So far, more than 100 jurisdictions have been involved in this reform process and have mainly considered four substantive provisions: indirect expropriation, FET, FPS and MFN treatment [88]. In addition, efforts have also been made to discuss two approaches that governments could use to transit earlier treaties towards newer designs, including issuing joint interpretations to clarify their intentions and concluding a plurilateral agreement to modify existing rights and obligations [88]. In 2025, the OCED, UNCITRAL and UNCTAD jointly organized an Investment Treaty Conference for states to further discuss and reflect on these substantive reforms[88].

## 6.4 Conclusion

Over the past two decades, the international investment law regime has experienced a profound legitimacy crisis. Amid the global backlash against investment arbitration, treaty reform efforts have been undertaken at the national, bilateral, regional, and multilateral levels. Current developments indicate that this backlash remains an ongoing process. While states continue to demonstrate divergent approaches to investment treaty making, multilateral forums such as OECD and UNCITRAL have emerged as crucial platforms for deliberating both substantive and procedural reforms. Although several agreements have been reached on individual reform issues, the broader reform process still faces significant challenges and remains unfinished.

## References

1. M. Sornarajah (2008) A Coming Crisis: Expansionary Trends in Investment Treaty Arbitration. In: Karl P. Sauvant (ed) Appeals Mechanism in International Investment Disputes. Oxford, pp. 39–79
2. Técnicas Medioambientales Tecmed, S.A. v. The United Mexican States, ICSID Case No. ARB (AF)/00/2
3. Spain-Mexico BIT (1996)
4. Occidental Petroleum Corporation and Occidental Exploration and Production Company v. The Republic of Ecuador, ICSID Case No. ARB/06/11

5. Kenneth. J. Vandevelde (2009) A Comparison of the 2004 and 1994 U.S. Model BITs: Rebalancing Investor and Host Country Interests. In: Karl. P. Sauvant (ed), Yearbook on International Investment Law & Policy 2008–2009. Oxford, pp. 283–316
6. NAFTA Free Trade Commission Notes of Interpretation of Certain Chapter 11 Provisions (2001)
7. Pope & Talbot Inc. v. The Government of Canada, UNCITRAL 1976
8. Anthony Depalma (2001) Nafta's Powerful Little Secrete; Obscure Tribunals Settle Disputes, but Go Too Far, Critics Say, New York Times. https://www.nytimes.com/2001/03/11/business/nafta-s-powerful-little-secret-obscure-tribunals-settle-disputes-but-go-too-far.html. Accessed 18 August 2025
9. United States Model BIT (2004)
10. Canada Model BIT (2004)
11. Methanex Corporation v. United States of America, UNCITRAL 1976
12. M. Sornarajah (2015) Resistance and Change in the International Law on Foreign Investment. Cambridge, United Kingdom
13. US-Argentina BIT (1991)
14. Jose E. Alvarez (2010) Why Are We "Re-calibrating" Our Investment Treaties. World Arbitration & Mediation Review. Volume 4, Issue 2: 143–161
15. Nathalie Bernasconi-Osterwalder (2016) Giving Arbitrators carte blanche–Fair and Equitable Treatment in Investment Treaties. In: C. L. Lim (ed), Alternative Visions of the International Law on Foreign Investment: Essays in Honour of Muthucumaraswamy Sornarajah. Cambridge, pp. 324–348
16. Junqing Chao (2019) Addressing the Global Backlash against Investment Arbitration? A Multilateral Investment Agreement and China. China and WTO Review, Volume 5, Issue 2: 269–298
17. Charles N. Brower and Stephan W. Schill (2009) Is Arbitration a Threat or a Boon to the Legitimacy of International Investment Law?. Chicago Journal of International Law, Volume 9, Issue 2: 471–498
18. Michael Waibel, Asha Kaushal, Kyo-Hwa Liz Chung and Claire Balchin (eds) (2010) The Backlash against Investment Arbitration. Kluwer, London
19. Damon Vis-Dunbar, Luke Eric Peterson and Fernando Cabrera Diaz (2007) Bolivia Notifies World Bank of Withdrawal from ICSID, Pursues BIT Revisions. https://www.bilaterals.org/?bolivia-notifies-world-bank-of&lang=en. Accessed 18 August 2025
20. Bretton Woods Project (2009) ICSID in Crisis: Straight–Jacket or Investment Protection? https://www.brettonwoodsproject.org/2009/07/art-564878/. Accessed 18 August 2025
21. Ewan Robertson (2012) Venezuela Announces "Irrevocable" Withdrawal from World Bank's Arbitration Body. https://venezuelanalysis.com/news/6773/. Accessed 18 August 2025
22. UNCTAD (2010) Denunciation of the ICSID Convention and BITs: Impact on Investor-State Claims. Switzerland
23. Rosa Amilli Guzman Perez and Racha El Herfi (2012) Constitutional Court of Ecuador Decision on the Constitutionality of the BIT Ecuador-France. Transnational Dispute Settlement 3
24. Xavier Carim (2013) Lessons from South Africa's BITs Review. Columbia FDI Perspective No. 109. https://ccsi.columbia.edu/sites/ccsi.columbia.edu/files/content/docs/publications/No_109_-_Carim_-_FINAL.pdf. Accessed 18 August 2025
25. South Africa Protection of Investment Act 22 (2015)
26. David Prince (2016) Indonesia's Bold Strategy on Bilateral Investment Treaties: Seeking an Equitable Climate for Investment?. Asian Journal of International Law, Volume 7, Issue 1: 124–151
27. Antony Crockett (2015) Indonesia's Bilateral Investment Treaties: Between Generations?. ICSID Review, Volume 30, Issue 2: 437–448
28. Australian Government Department of Foreign Affairs and Trade (2011) Government Trade Policy Statement: Trading Our Way to More Jobs and Prosperity.
29. M. Sornarajah (2013) The Case against a Regime on International Investment Law. In: Leno E. Trakman and Nicola W. Ranieri (ed) Regionalism in International Investment Law. Oxford, pp. 475–498

30. Philip Morris Asia Limited v. The Commonwealth of Australia, UNCITRAL, PCA Case No. 2012-12
31. Jurgen Kurtz and Luke R. Nottage (2015) Investment Treaty Arbitration "Down Under": Policy and Politics in Australia. ICSID Review, Volume 30, Issue 2: pp. 465–480
32. Australia-Korea FTA (2014)
33. Australia-China FTA (2015)
34. Parliament of Australia (2015) Blind Agreement: Reforming Australia's Treaty-making Process. https://www.aph.gov.au/Parliamentary_Business/Committees/Senate/Foreign_Affairs_Defence_and_Trade/Treaty-making_process/~/media/Committees/fadt_ctte/Treaty-making_process/report.pdf. Accessed 18 August 2025
35. Australian Government Department of Foreign Affairs and Trade, Australia's bilateral investment treaties. https://www.dfat.gov.au/trade/investment/australias-bilateral-investment-treaties. Accessed 18 August 2025
36. Australia-United Arab Emirates Comprehensive Economic Partnership Agreement (2024)
37. UNCTAD (2015) World Investment Report 2015: Reforming International Investment Governance. Switzerland
38. Bipartisan Trade Promotion Authority Act (2022)
39. United States Model BIT (1994)
40. Jose E. Alvarez (2011) The Return of the State. Minnesota Journal of International Law, Volume 20, Issue 2: 223–264
41. M. Kantor (2012) Little Has Changed in the New US Model Bilateral Investment Treaty. ICSID Review, Volume 27, Issue 2: 335–378
42. The Treaty of Lisbon (2009)
43. Wenhua Shan and Sheng Zhang (2010) The Treaty of Lisbon: Half Way Toward a Common Investment Policy. European Journal of International Law, Volume 21, Issue 4: 1049–1073
44. European Commission (2010) Communication from the Commission to the European Parliament, the Council, the European Economic and Social Committee and the Committee of the Regions: Towards a Comprehensive European International Investment Policy
45. European Commission, Negotiations and Agreements. https://policy.trade.ec.europa.eu/eu-trade-relationships-country-and-region/negotiations-and-agreements_en. Accessed 18 August 2025
46. Christian J. Tams (2014) Procedural Aspects of Investor-State Dispute Settlement: The Emergence of a European Approach?. Journal of World Investment & Trade, Volume 15, Issue 3-4: 585–611
47. European Commission (2014) Questions and Answers: Public Online Consultation on Investor Protection in TTIP. https://ec.europa.eu/commission/presscorner/api/files/document/print/en/memo_14_206/MEMO_14_206_EN.pdf. Accessed 18 August 2025
48. European Commission (2015) Report Online public consultation on investment protection and investor-to-state dispute settlement (ISDS) in the Transatlantic Trade and Investment Partnership Agreement (TTIP). https://www.europarl.europa.eu/meetdocs/2014_2019/documents/inta/dv/swd(2015)0003final_/swd(2015)0003final_en.pdf. Accessed 18 August 2025
49. European Commission (2015) Investment in TTIP and Beyond–the Path for Reform: Enhancing the Right to Regulate and Moving from Current Ad Hoc Arbitration Towards an Investment Court
50. European Commission (2017) Inception Impact Assessment–Establishment of a Multilateral Investment Court for Investment Dispute Resolution. https://ec.europa.eu/smart-regulation/roadmaps/docs/2016_trade_024_court_on_investment_en.pdf. Accessed 18 August 2025
51. European Commission, Multilateral Investment Court Project. https://policy.trade.ec.europa.eu/enforcement-and-protection/multilateral-investment-court-project_en. Accessed 11 August 2025
52. EU-Canada Comprehensive Economic and Trade Agreement (2016)
53. European Commission, Investment. https://policy.trade.ec.europa.eu/help-exporters-and-importers/accessing-markets/investment_en. Accessed 7 August 2025
54. India Model BIT (2015)

55. Prabhash Ranjan (2014) India and Bilateral Investment Treaties–A Changing Landscape, ICSID Review, Volume 29, Issue 2: 419–450
56. White Industries Australia Limited v. The Republic of India, UNCITRAL
57. Grant Hanessian and Kabir Duggal (2015) The Final 2015 Indian Model BIT: Is This Change the World Wishes to See?. ICSID Review, Volume 32, Issue 1: 216–226
58. C.L. Lim, Deborah Kay Elms and Patrick Low (eds) (2012) The Trans-Pacific Partnership: A Quest for a Twenty-first Century Trade Agreement. Cambridge
59. Trans-Pacific Partnership (2016)
60. Comprehensive and Progressive Agreement for Trans-Pacific Partnership (2018)
61. Regional Comprehensive Economic Partnership (2020)
62. China-Korea BIT (2007)
63. China-Japan-Korea Trilateral Investment Agreement (2012)
64. China-Korea FTA (2015)
65. Sungjin Kang (2017) Conflict of Investment-Related Provisions under Regional Trade Agreements between Korea and China–Navigating the "Noodle Bowl". ICSID Review, Volume 32, Issue 2: 418–430
66. UNCTAD (2020) International Investment Agreements Reform Accelerator. Switzerland
67. UNCITRAL Rules on Transparency in Treaty-based Investor-State Arbitration (2014)
68. Anthea Roberts and Taylor St John (2022) UNCITRAL and ISDS Reform: What to Expect When You're Expecting. Blog of the European Journal of International Law. https://www.ejiltalk.org/uncitral-and-isds-reform-what-to-expect-when-youre-expecting/. Accessed 18 August 2025
69. Anthea Roberts and Taylor St John (2023) UNCITRAL and ISDS Reform: Moving to the Delivery Phase. Blog of the European Journal of International Law. https://www.ejiltalk.org/uncitral-and-isds-reform-moving-to-the-delivery-phase/. Accessed 11 August 2025
70. UNCITRAL (2024) UNCITRAL Working Group III Concludes Its Work on the Draft Statute of an Advisory Centre on International Investment Dispute Resolution. https://unis.unvienna.org/unis/pressrels/2024/unisl355.html. Accessed 18 August 2025
71. UNCITRAL Working Group III (2024) A/CN.9/WG.III/WP.239—Possible reform of investor-State dispute settlement (ISDS): Draft statute of a standing mechanism for the resolution of international investment disputes. https://docs.un.org/en/A/CN.9/WG.III/WP.239. Accessed 11 August 2025
72. UNCITRAL Working Group III (2024) A/CN.9/WG.III/WP.249—Summary of the intersessional meeting on investor-State dispute settlement (ISDS) reform submitted by the Government of the People's Republic of China. https://docs.un.org/en/A/CN.9/WG.III/WP.249. Accessed 11 August 2025
73. UNCITRAL Working Group III (2025) A/CN.9/WG.III/WP.256—Possible reform of investor-State dispute settlement (ISDS): Structure and design of a standing mechanism for the resolution of international investment disputes. https://docs.un.org/en/A/CN.9/WG.III/WP.256. Accessed 11 August 2025
74. ICSID, ICSID Rules and Regulations Amendment. https://icsid.worldbank.org/resources/rules-amendments. Accessed 18 August 2025
75. ICSID, About the ICSID Rule Amendments. https://icsid.worldbank.org/resources/rules-and-regulations/amendments/about. Accessed 18 August 2025
76. Meg Kinnear (2022) The Launch of a New Generation of the ICSID Rules. Columbia FDI Perspectives, No. 326. https://ccsi.columbia.edu/sites/ccsi.columbia.edu/files/content/docs/fdi%20perspectives/No%20326%20-%20Kinnear%20-%20FINAL.pdf. Accessed 18 August 2025
77. Havana Charter (1948)
78. Multilateral Agreement on Investment Draft Text (1998)
79. The World Economic Forum (2013) Foreign Direct Investment as a Key Driver for Trade, Growth and Prosperity: The Case for a Multilateral Agreement on Investment. https://www3.weforum.org/docs/GAC13/WEF_GAC_GlobalTradeFDI_FDIKeyDriver_Report_2013.pdf. Accessed 18 August 2025

80. Karl P. Sauvant and Federico Ortino (2013) Improving the International Investment Law and Policy Regime: Options for the Future. http://wordpress.ei.columbia.edu/vcc/files/2014/03/Improving-The-International-Investment-Law-and-Policy-Regime-Options-for-the-Future-Sept-2013.pdf. Accessed 18 August 2025
81. Karl P. Sauvant (2023) The new WTO Investment Facilitation for Development Agreement. Columbia FDI Perspectives, No. 363. https://ccsi.columbia.edu/sites/ccsi.columbia.edu/files/content/docs/fdi%20perspectives/No%20363%20-%20Sauvant%20-%20FINAL.pdf. Accessed 18 August 2025
82. EU-Singapore FTA (2018)
83. EU-Viet Nam FTA (2019)
84. United States-Mexico-Canada Agreement (2018)
85. United States Trade Representative (2017) Summary of Objectives for the NAFTA Renegotiation. https://ustr.gov/sites/default/files/files/Press/Releases/NAFTAObjectives.pdf. Accessed 11 August 2025
86. Brazil Cooperation and Facilitation Investment Agreement (2015)
87. Nicolas M. Perrone and Guastavo Rojas de Cerqueira Cesar (2015) Brazil's Bilateral Investment Treaties: More Than a New Investment Treaty Model? Columbia FDI Perspective No. 159. https://ccsi.columbia.edu/sites/ccsi.columbia.edu/files/content/docs/publications/No-159-Perrone-and-Ce%cc%81sar-FINAL.pdf. Accessed 18 August 2025
88. OECD, Modernising investment treaties (Track 2). https://www.oecd.org/en/topics/sub-issues/the-future-of-investment-treaties/modernising-investment-treaties.html. Accessed 18 August 2025

# Chapter 7
# The Fourth Generation of Chinese Investment Treaties and Investment Treaty Reform

This chapter examines the broader implications of China's fourth-generation investment treaties for the ongoing investment treaty reforms. As established earlier, these reforms have been implemented at the national, bilateral, regional and multilateral levels. Within this context, China's fourth-generation treaties may provide significant contributions to reform initiatives across all levels. The chapter addresses three key questions: (1) how China's fourth-generation investment treaties constitute an emerging model in the balancing debate at the national level (Sect. 7.1); (2) how China has pursed treaty consolidation at the bilateral and regional levels (Sect. 7.2); and (3) how China has actively participated in multilateral investment rulemaking (Sect. 7.3). The chapter concludes with a comprehensive assessment of China's evolving role in international investment governance (Sect. 7.4).

## 7.1 Emerging China's Model in the Balancing Debate

As discussed in Chap. 6, many states have reformulated their investment treaties under the global backlash against investment arbitration. Most of them, notably the US, the EU, India as well as China, aim at striking a balance between investment protection and the right of states to regulate. As discussed in Chap. 3, China's investment treaties have become more balanced over the past decade, learning from the US experience—particularly the 2004 US Model BIT [1]. In contrast, the US, EU and India have primarily learned from their experiences in investment arbitration and have proposed certain new balancing approaches. For example, the formulation of the minimum standard of treatment in the 2004 US Model BIT was largely built upon the FTC's Interpretation Note [2, 3]. Additionally, the exclusion of the MFN clause in the 2015 Indian Model BIT partly resulted from the *White Industries v. India* case [4, 5].



J. Chao, *The Emerging Fourth Generation of Chinese Investment Treaties*,
https://doi.org/10.1007/978-981-95-5052-4_7

Considering this, it may be premature to claim that China's fourth-generation investment treaties will significantly contribute to the national level of investment treaty reforms. However, China's learning process may contribute to the consolidation of investment treaty rules. For example, China and the EU in their negotiations may reach a consensus on some issues, such as the clarification of indirect expropriation. China's contribution to treaty consolidation at the bilateral and regional levels will be discussed in the next section. This section aims to compare the specific balanced provisions of China, the US, the EU, and India to identify their similarities and differences. The findings could serve as a basis for further treaty consolidation.

Regarding China's balancing practice, since China has not released an official new Model BIT, this section examines the emerging fourth generation of Chinese investment treaties as discussed in Chaps. 2–5. For the US balancing practice, attention is given to the 2012 US Model BIT. This section will also examine the investment chapter of the 2018 USMCA, which differs from the 2012 US Model BIT in some respects and may represent the US new attitude towards investment protection. When examining the EU's balancing practice, the 2016 CETA will be the focus, with reference to the EU's other FTAs. The 2015 Indian Model BIT will represent India's balancing approach.

Regarding the specific balanced provisions, six clauses will be selected and examined: (1) definitions of investment and investor; (2) national treatment and MFN treatment; (3) the FET and FPS standards; (4) indirect expropriation; (5) exception clauses; and (6) the ISDS mechanism. According to UNCTAD, these provisions contribute to the reform objectives of preserving regulatory space of host states and reforming the exiting ISDS mechanism [6]. Furthermore, the preamble of investment treaties will also be examined, as it determines the treaty's objectives.

### *7.1.1 Preamble*

Although the 2004 and 2012 US Model BITs adopted a balanced approach, it was not until the 2018 USMCA that the right of states to regulate was explicitly affirmed in the treaty preamble [2, 7, 8]. Specifically, USMCA goes beyond prior agreements by not only employing the phrase "inherent right to regulate" but also providing an extensive list of legitimate public policy objectives [8]. Similarly, the preamble of the 2015 Indian Model BIT reaffirms the right of states to regulate for public policy [4]. Through these reaffirmations, the US and India both seek to guide arbitral tribunals in treaty interpretation.

In contrast, the EU's investment treaties adopt a two-pronged approach, combining a reaffirmation of the right of states to regulate in their preambles with dedicated provisions on investment and regulatory measures, as exemplified by the 2016 CETA [9]. Notably, the CETA stipulates that the negative impact of regulatory measures on investor expectations or a decision not to grant a subsidy, does not, in itself, constitute a treaty breach [9, 10]. Regarding China's approach, neither the 2012 China-Canada BIT nor the 2012 China-Japan- Korea TIT reaffirms the right of states to regulate in its preamble [11, 12]. However, subsequent agreements demonstrate evolving practice, as evidenced in the 2013 China-Tanzania BIT, 2015 China-Australia FTA, and 2020 RCEP [13–15].

In summary, all four states (the US, EU, China, and India) have incorporated explicit reaffirmations of the right of states to regulate in the preambles of their recent investment treaties. This common practice reflects an emerging international consensus in contemporary investment treaty reform. The key divergence, however, lies in the specific balancing mechanisms adopted by each state to operationalize this principle within their respective treaty frameworks.

### *7.1.2 Definitions of Investment and Investor*

As discussed in Chap. 3, there are two main approaches to clarify the definition of investment: the first incorporates the Salini test and specifies the characteristics that an investment must fulfill while the second excludes certain types of assets from the definition of investment [16].

For the first approach, the US and China adopt the same method, requiring three characteristics: capital commitment, profit expectation, and risk assumption [8, 14]. The EU introduces an additional characteristic—certain duration—while India includes one more: development contribution [4, 9]. The UNCTAD recognizes that these additional characteristics contribute to the sustainable development of international investment law [16].

For the second approach, the US and the EU exclude two types of assets: claims arising solely from commercial contracts and judicial or administrative awards [8, 9]. China adds exclusions for sovereign debt and for market share or opportunities [15]. In contrast, India provides a non-exhaustive list of exclusions that incorporates all the aforementioned types and other claims lacking substantive investment characteristics [4]. The UNCTAD notes that these exclusions are typically introduced in response to arbitral practice [16].

Regarding the definition of investor, the US, EU (e.g., under the 2016 CETA), China and India all stipulate that legal entities must carry (substantial) business activities to qualify, thereby excluding shell companies [4, 8, 9, 14]. The 2018 EU-Singapore investment agreement further requires entities to both operate substantive business activities and maintain their seat in the host state [17]. Additionally, the US, EU, and India address dual nationality, whereas China has not yet adopted similar provisions [4, 8, 9].

### *7.1.3 National Treatment and Most-Favored-Nation Treatment*

The US, EU, China, and India all explicitly provide that national treatment applies only in "like circumstances" [4, 8, 9, 15]. As discussed in Chap. 3, this clarification addresses prior arbitral awards where tribunals extended national treatment even in the absence of comparable conditions [16]. The US, China, and India further list specific factors for assessing "like circumstances", enhancing legal predictability [4, 8, 15]. However, India excludes the MFN treatment from its 2015 Model BIT [4]. As noted, this exclusion partly resulted from its investment arbitration experience, particularly the *White Industries v. India* case. Additionally, the EU and China expressly preclude the MFN clause from being applied to dispute settlement provisions [9, 11].

### *7.1.4 Fair and Equitable Treatment and Full Protection and Security*

As discussed in Chap. 3, there are two main approaches to clarify the scope of the FET and FPS standards: the first one is a non-exhaustive list approach, adopted by the US and China while the second one is an exhaustive/closed list approach, adopted by the EU and India [4, 8, 9, 11]. The main difference lies in that the elements listed in a non-exhaustive way serve as examples for tribunals' consideration while as to the elements in the exhaustive/closed list, tribunals can only consider and cannot go beyond these elements. The UNCTAD notes that the exhaustive/closed list approach could help prevent expansive treaty interpretations by arbitral tribunals, but reaching consensus on such a list would be challenging [16].

A closer examination of the 2015 Indian Model BIT and the 2016 CETA shows that the exhaustive/closed list approach has been adopted differently in several aspects. First, compared to the CETA, the Indian Model BIT provides a shorter list of elements for tribunals to consider [4, 9]. Second, the CETA does not contain any reference while the Indian Model BIT refers the FET standard to customary international law [4, 9]. Third, unlike the Indian Model BIT, the CETA permits tribunals to consider additional FET elements, provided they are developed by the Committee on Services and Investment and approved by the CETA Joint Committee [4, 9]. Fourth, the CETA explicitly clarifies that legitimate expectations do not constitute an independent element of the FET standard, but may only be considered as a relevant factor when evaluating the specifically listed FET elements [9, 10].

It is important to note that while recent Chinese investment treaties have drawn from the US experience by adopting the non-exhaustive list approach, China may need to consider the EU's exhaustive/closed list approach—particularly in their ongoing negotiations. China's final position on the FET clarification remains uncertain in its fourth-generation investment treaties. Additionally, it remains unclear how the exhaustive/closed list approach will be interpreted in arbitral practice and whether this approach will effectively constrain expansive interpretations by tribunals.

### 7.1.5 Indirect Expropriation

The US, EU, China, and India share relatively consistent practice in clarifying indirect expropriation. These clarifications primarily include (1) listing considerations in determining indirect expropriation; and (2) including exceptions for non-discriminatory regulatory measures adopted for legitimate public policy objectives [4, 8, 9, 15].

Regarding the first clarification, the US and China adopt a three-factor test that requires an assessment of a regulatory measure's nature, economic impact and interference with reasonable expectations—while the EU and India employ a four-factor test, adding the duration of these measures [4, 8, 9, 15]. Similar to the practice regarding investment definition, the EU and India place greater emphasis on "duration". Furthermore, India exhibits caution regarding the factor of investment expectation, by replacing it with the more specific requirement of a "prior binding written commitment" [4].

The second clarification concerns expropriation exception. All four states agree that non-discriminatory regulatory measures adopted for legitimate public policy objectives should not constitute indirect expropriation, except in the rare circumstances [4, 8, 9, 15]. Regarding the "rare circumstances", the EU (e.g., under the 2016 CETA) explains that they occur when the impact of a measure is "manifestly excessive" relative to its purpose [9]. In contrast, China (e.g., under the 2012 China-Canada BIT) defines them by assessing whether the severity of a measure indicates a lack of good faith [11]. As for other major models, the 2012 US Model BIT includes the term but does not define it, whereas the 2015 Indian Model omits it entirely [4, 7].

As noted by UNCTAD, these two clarifications, while not eliminating liability risks, serve to balance the interests of host states and investors [16]. A more restrictive approach is to explicitly exclude indirect expropriation from ISDS provisions or treaty coverage. For example, the US under the 2018 USMCA limits foreign investors to challenging only breaches of direct expropriation, thereby excluding indirect expropriation claims [8]. Additionally, the 2020 India-Brazil Investment Cooperation and Facilitation Treaty only convers direct expropriation [18].

### 7.1.6 Exception Clauses

To safeguard the right of states to regulate, one of the most effective strategies is the incorporation of exception clauses. According to UNCTAD, these clauses generally fall into two categories: (1) national security exceptions; and (2) public policy exceptions [6]. The US, EU, China, and India all incorporate both types in their investment treaties [4, 7, 9, 11].

National security exceptions are typically self-judging, as exemplified by the 2012 US Model BIT [6, 7]. Public policy exceptions, meanwhile, commonly cover areas such as environmental protection, financial services regulation, information security, and cultural preservation [16]. Investment treaties often specify the applicable standards, such as a self-judging test for environmental protection and a non-discrimination requirement for financial services [4, 7].

### *7.1.7 ISDS Mechanism*

In the context of ISDS reform, Roberts in 2017 categorized states into four groups: "loyalists", "reformists", "revolutionaries"; and "undecideds" [19]. Specifically, she argued that:

(1) the US generally represented the "loyalists" position, advocating for "incremental reform" [19]. This was evident in the progressive improvements seen in the 2004 and 2012 US Model BITs [2, 7]. However, it is noteworthy that the 2018 USMCA applies ISDS provisions only to Mexico-US investment disputes and imposes significant limitations on ISDS provisions [8]. The US final position on ISDS reform remains uncertain, reflecting a potential shift from its "loyalists" stance toward an "undecideds" position.
(2) the EU exemplified the "reformists" approach, pushing for more fundamental, institutional changes [19]. This was most clearly demonstrated by its multilateral investment court proposal—a systemic alternative to traditional ISDS mechanism. As discussed in Chap. 6, Canada, Vietnam, and Singapore have agreed to adopt the investment court system [9, 17, 20]. The investment court is also one of the key issues in the EU-China BIT negotiations. To date, the EU has consistently maintained its "reformists" position.
(3) China fell into the "undecideds" category, as it developed its investment treaty framework on "an incremental, case-by-case basis" [19]. The inconsistent practice and underlying rationale of China's fourth-generation investment treaties has been extensively analyzed in Chaps 3–5. More significantly, as discussed in Chap. 4, China signaled a policy shift in 2019 by submitting a proposal for ISDS reform at UNCITRAL Working Group III, advocating for establishing a WTO-style multilateral appellate mechanism to complement the existing investment arbitration system [21]. This evolving position was further demonstrated in 2024 when China hosted an UNCITRAL intersessional meeting in Chengdu to discuss the key issues of the appellate mechanism [22]. These developments indicate China's gradual transition from "undecideds" to "reformists" stance.

(4) India was similarly categorized among the "undecideds", as the 2015 Indian Model BIT largely limits foreign investors' access to international arbitration—particularly by imposing a five-year domestic remedies exhaustion requirement [19]. Furthermore, the 2015 Indian Model BIT considers establishing an appeal body to enhance the coherence of treaty interpretations while outlining key considerations for such a body [19]. As discussed in Chap. 6, India's cautious approach to investment protection stems largely from its negative experience in recent investment arbitration cases. Some Indian scholars have expressed dissatisfaction with this restrictive model [23]. It remains to be seen whether India will further modify its investment treaty policy.

In summary, while the US, the EU, China, and India all explicitly reaffirm states' regulatory rights in their treaty preambles, they adopt different approaches to specific balanced provisions. The key challenges center on clarifying the FET and FPS standards and advancing the ISDS reform. These differences may be resolved through bilateral and regional investment treaty negotiations or under multilateral reform platforms, such as UNCITRAL for ISDS reform and OECD for substantive provision reform.

## 7.2 Finding Consensus Under the Bilateral and Regional Treaties

As discussed previously, although China has yet to propose new balanced provisions, it has been watching and learning from other states' experiences. Such a strategy could facilitate treaty consolidation under ongoing investment treaty reforms. As examined in Chap. 5, in recent years, China has concluded investment treaties with key partners, including the ASEAN in 2009, Japan and Korea in 2012, Canada in 2012, and Australia in 2015. More importantly, China signed the RECP in 2020 and formally applied to join the CPTPP in 2021. These treaties provide a platform for states to collectively reflect on investment treaty reform. Consequently, this section will compare how the 2018 CPTPP and 2020 RCEP strike a balance between investment protection and the right of states to regulate. The objective is to determine whether these two mega-FTAs share any consensus on balanced provisions.

First, both treaties in their preambles reaffirm the right of states to regulate [15, 24]. Second, regarding specific substantive protection provisions, both treaties stipulate that investments should fulfill three key characteristics: capital commitment, profit expectation, and risk assumption [15, 24]. Additionally, they share two identical exclusions of assets: judicial or administrative judgments, and sovereign debts[15, 24]. Furthermore, RCEP introduces two additional exclusions: claims solely from commercial contracts and market share or opportunities [15]. As for the definition of investor, both treaties require legal entities to demonstrate that they have undertaken substantial business activities in the host states but do not address dual nationality for natural persons[15, 24].

Furthermore, both treaties explicitly provide that national treatment and MFN treatment apply only under "like circumstances" and that MFN clause does not apply to procedural provisions [15, 24]. Additionally, they adopt nearly identical approaches in clarifying the FET and FPS standards (by the non-exhaustive list approach) and in clarifying indirect expropriation (outlining factors for determination and establishing exceptions for non-discriminatory measures) [15, 24]. CPTPP further clarifies the scope of FET and FPS obligations by specifying that the mere act of issuing, renewing, or maintaining a subsidy or grant shall not be considered a violation of these obligations [24]. Moreover, both treaties incorporate exceptions for national security and public policy, particularly in areas concerning environmental protection, financial services regulation, and information security [15, 24].

Third, regarding procedural provisions, as discussed in Chap. 4, CPTPP advocates for the existing ISDS mechanism with certain enhancements. For example, it explicitly addresses several issues in arbitral proceedings—including arbitrator selection, amicus curiae submissions, preliminary objections, burden of proof, interim measures, governing law, arbitral transparency, and claim consolidation—to promote a fairer and more efficient dispute settlement mechanism [24]. Additionally, it expands the involvement of the contracting states in arbitral proceedings—including through non-disputing party's submissions on treaty interpretation [24]. In contrast, RCEP defers ISDS provisions for future negotiations [15]. Notably, two RCEP member states—Singapore and Vietnam—have agreed to adopt the investment court system in their investment treaties with the EU [17, 20]. However, these two states are also CPTPP members that advocate for traditional investment arbitration. Consequently, it remains uncertain how RCEP will ultimately structure its ISDS mechanism.

To conclude, CPTPP and RCEP demonstrate significant convergence on substantive provisions in the balancing debate, including their preambles, definitions of investment and investor, national treatment, MFN treatment, FET and FPS standards, indirect expropriation, and exception clauses. This convergence suggests that these treaties have strong potential to foster harmonization in substantive balanced provisions—a development that can provide a solid foundation for OECD's moderation work in this area. The core challenge, however, remains the ISDS reform. As stated above, the ISDS reform has been advanced at UNCITRAL, with most CPTPP and RCEP member states actively participating. The RCEP's silence on ISDS provisions may reflect that contracting states still maintain divergent views on the ISDS reform. However, as UNCITRAL's reform process progresses, it is expected that a consensus on procedural frameworks may eventually emerge.

## 7.3 Promoting Discussions on Multilateral Investment Rules

As discussed in Chaps. 4 and 6, multilateral efforts to reform investment rules have advanced on two platforms: UNCITRAL has focused on the ISDS reform, while the OECD has led discussions on modernizing substantive protection provisions. China has actively engaged in both initiatives—particularly submitting its own reform proposal at UNCITRAL. Beyond these forums, China has also promoted discussions on multilateral investment rules within the G20 and WTO. The details of these efforts will be examined in the following sections.

### *7.3.1 G20 Guiding Principles for Global Investment Policymaking*

In 2016, the G20 under China's presidency established a Trade and Investment Working Group, and one of its achievements was the Guiding Principles for Global Investment Policymaking (G20 Guiding Principles) [25]. The non-binding G20 Guiding Principles offer a framework for investment policymaking across core areas, including investment environment, protection, regulation, promotion, and facilitation [25, 26]. The G20 Guiding Principles has been highlighted by the UNCTAD as the first multilateral consensus on investment rules and viewed by scholars as a crucial step toward structuring a future multilateral investment framework [27, 28].

However, it has been found that these principles are overly general. For example, Principle VI merely recognizes the right of states to regulate without providing further elaboration [27]. As discussed above, this is a shared consensus under the investment treaty reform, and as discussed previously, four G20 countries— including the US, EU, China, and India—have reaffirmed this principle in the preambles of their investment treaties. The key point is that these four states have balanced investment protection with the right of states to regulate to varying degrees. The main problems lie in the clarification of the FET and FPS standards and the reform of the ISDS mechanism. Furthermore, as discussed in Chap. 6, other G20 countries hold differing views on dispute settlement mechanism, such as Brazil's proposal of the dispute prevention mechanism and South Africa's use of domestic mediation mechanism. Sauvant argued that the general language of the G20 Guiding Principles represented a compromise [28].

Despite this progress, investment facilitation could be advanced. In recent years, investment facilitation has increasingly attracted public attention and has been substantially discussed at UNCTAD and OECD [29–31]. The investment facilitation discussions were also launched at the 2016 G20 Summit, but unfortunately no results were achieved [28]. The G20 trade ministers in their declaration called for continued efforts to advance investment facilitation for the purpose of economic development [32]. The 2017 G20 under Germany's presidency proposed "a non-binding investment facilitation package", which was opposed by some states such as India [33]. Fortunately, however, discussions on investment facilitation have been advanced at the WTO.

### *7.3.2 WTO Investment Facilitation for Development Agreement*

In April 2017, the Friends of Investment Facilitation for Development (FIFD), a group including China, was established at the WTO to advance this agenda [34]. China also submitted an Investment Facilitation Communication for members' consideration [35, 36]. Meanwhile, Mexico, Indonesia, Korea and other states launched a workshop, demonstrating their recognition of the WTO's important role in investment and their willingness to engage in related discussions [37].

It is noteworthy that although WTO investment negotiations under the Doha Round collapsed due to opposition from developing countries, it is these countries that are now proactively proposing new discussions on investment facilitation [38]. This shift in stance mainly stems from three key considerations: (1) a growing recognition of the interdependence between trade and investment [34, 38]; (2) their emergence as significant capital exporters with increasing OFDI interests [38]; and (3) despite their OFDI growth, their continued reliance on substantial FDI inflows for economic development [38–40].

China's Investment Facilitation Communication focused on three aspects. First, it emphasized enhancing transparency in the investment policy framework. It proposed that (1) all relevant laws and regulations, including new measures, should be open to the public; (2) enquiry points should be established to address reasonable enquiries by foreign investors; and (3) in compliance with domestic laws and regulations and as far as practical, stakeholders should be afforded opportunities to provide comments on proposed laws and regulations [35].

Second, the Communication highlighted the importance of streamlining administrative procedures for investment activities. It proposed that (1) states should establish clear and consistent procedures for investment approvals; (2) states should clearly specify the required documents for investment applications and allow foreign investors to submit additional information where applications were incomplete; and (3) states should enhance institutional cooperation and coordination with other states [35].

Third, the Communication emphasized addressing the special needs of developing and least-developed countries. It recommended providing (1) special and differential treatments to accommodate their needs; and (2) technical assistance to enhance their capacity [35]. Additionally, it encouraged foreign investors to undertake corporate social responsibilities in the host states [35]. Overall, China's Investment Facilitation Communication presented a comprehensive framework for the WTO members' consideration and deliberation.

In August 2017, China also facilitated the adoption of the Outlines for BRICS Investment Facilitation (BRICS Outlines) at the Summit [41]. Subsequently, at the WTO 11th Ministerial Conference in December 2017, while investment facilitation was not included in the negotiation agenda, 41 members and the EU called for establishing a multilateral framework focusing on transparent and predictable investment measures, streamlined administrative procedures, and enhanced international cooperation and exchange [42]. These elements aligned substantially with both China's Investment Facilitation Communication and the BRICS Outlines.

After six years of negotiations, the IFD agreement was eventually finalized in February 2024, with 126 members seeking to incorporate it into the WTO framework as a plurilateral agreement [39]. The IFD agreement establishes provisions in five key areas:

(1) Enhancing the transparency of investment measures: the IFD agreement requires that investment-related measures and information should be published without imposing any fees. If a state requires that foreign investments must be authorized, it should publish the requirement and procedures for such authorization. States are also encouraged to establish a single information portal for publication. Additionally, in compliance with domestic laws and regulations and as far as practical, states should publish proposed measures in advance and offer interested people opportunities to comment on these measures [43].
(2) Streamlining and speeding up administrative procedures: the IFD agreement first establishes a general principle—stating that all regulatory measures should be administrated reasonably, objectively and impartially. Then it addresses investment authorization, with provisions on several key aspects: the general principle that states shall avoid undue burdens and delays, the procedures covering application period, requirements, acceptance of authenticated copies, treatment of incomplete applications, handling of multiple applications, as well as the requirement that authorization fees be reasonable and transparent. It also stressed that authorization authorities should be independent [43].
(3) Establishing focal points to respond to foreign investors' enquiries, assisting foreign investors to obtain relevant information, and promoting the coherence of domestic regulatory measures [43].
(4) Providing special and differential treatment for developing and least-developed countries [43].
(5) Promoting sustainable investment, including encouraging responsible business conduct and adopting measures against business corruption [43].

Overall, the WTO IFD agreement has some overlaps with China's Investment Facilitation Communication but is more comprehensive. Beyond being praised as the first multilateral rule on investment, its rapid conclusion serves as a key demonstration that the WTO is still able to achieve concrete outcomes [44]

## 7.4 China's Evolving Role in International Investment Governance

Over the past decade, one of the most frequently explored issues has been the role China has played in international investment governance—whether it is a rule taker, rule breaker or rule maker? For example, Berger argued that although China had been actively involved in international investment governance, it still acted as a rule taker, because it largely relied on the partner countries' templates for investment agreement negotiations and submitted only a limited number of investment facilitation proposals which were less comprehensive than those made by other WTO members including Brazil and the EU [45]. In contrast, Baetens and Zhang were more optimistic, arguing that with its growing economic power, China had started to adopt its own approach to investment protection and had emerged as a rule maker in international investment governance [46].

However, this issue cannot be answered with a single overall conclusion, because, as discussed in previous chapters, the emerging fourth generation of Chinese investment treaties cover four aspects, including investment liberalization, substantive investment protection, ISDS mechanism and investment facilitation. Therefore, this section will analyze this question in each of these aspects.

First, regarding investment liberalization, as discussed in Chap. 2, Chinese investment treaties did not incorporate the core provisions—pre-establishment national treatment and negative list approach—until the 2020 RCEP and the 2020 CAI [15, 47]. In fact, this shift was first advanced under the China-US BIT negotiations and was subsequently coupled with a fundamental liberalization in China's foreign investment regulatory regime. Furthermore, the 2020 CAI has prompted China to adopt comprehensive treaty commitments on other liberalization provisions, including absolute market access obligations, SOE disciplines, prohibitions on performance requirements, and sustainable development issues (such as regulatory transparency, environmental protection, labor rights and responsible corporate conduct) [47]. Therefore, it is fair to say that China has acted as a rule-taker in the field of investment liberalization.

Second, regarding substantive investment protection, as discussed in Chap. 3, recent Chinese investment treaties have balanced investment protection with the right of states to regulate, but this balancing practice has learned from the US experience and the global best practices in investment treaty reform [1]. This is evident in two key developments: (1) the clarification of key treaty provisions, such as the FET and FPS standards and indirect exploration; and (2) the incorporation of new exception clauses to safeguard legitimate public policy objectives. Furthermore, China's balancing practice exhibits two distinctive features: (1) progressive reform of treaty provisions; and (2) inconsistent application of these reforms. Therefore, China has still acted as a rule-taker in reforming substantive protection provisions. This role is understandable, however, given that China faced a surge in investment arbitration cases until recently, and as discussed in Chap. 4, most of these cases have centered on jurisdictional issues.

Third, regarding the ISDS mechanism, as discussed in Chap. 4, China followed the US practice from 2008 to 2015 in seeking to refine ISDS provisions [1, 2, 11]. However, after 2015, given growing criticisms on the ISDS mechanism and divergent reform proposals, China has begun to re-evaluate the existing ISDS mechanism. Eventually, in 2019, China submitted a proposal for ISDS reform at UNCITRAL Working Group III [21]. A closer examination shows that the hybrid approach in China's ISDS reform proposal—an ad hoc investment arbitration plus a WTO-style appellate mechanism—was largely built upon its domestic arbitration practice and thus differed from the conventional understanding of international arbitration. This can help explain why some international scholars felt quite confused when this hybrid approach was first published [48]. Subsequently, in October 2024, China hosted an UNCITRAL intersessional meeting in Chengdu to discuss the key issues of the appellate mechanism [22]. Considering these developments, China is more appropriately characterized as a rule-promoter rather than a rule-maker in ISDS reform.

Fourth, regarding investment facilitation, while Berger argued that China's proposal was less comprehensive than those made by other WTO members [45], the above analysis reveals substantial overlaps between the WTO IFD agreement and China's Investment Facilitation Communication—including enhanced regulatory transparency, streamlined administrative procedures as well as special and differential treatment for developing and least-developed countries. More significantly, the WTO discussions on investment facilitation were initially proposed by the FIFD group, which included China. Furthermore, before the WTO discussions, the G20 and the BRICS Summit under China's presidency had already begun to discuss investment facilitation and had even reached consensus on some key issues, as reflected in the G20 Guiding Principles and the BRICS Outlines [25, 41]. It is fair to say that these consensuses served as a solid foundation for developing and finalizing the WTO IFD agreement. These developments collectively demonstrate that China has emerged as a rule-maker in the field of investment facilitation.

## 7.5 Conclusion

China's fourth-generation investment treaties offer significant contributions to ongoing investment treaty reforms at the national, bilateral, regional, and multilateral levels. First, these treaties provide a China's model for balancing investment protection with the right of states to regulate. Second, China has pursued treaty consolidation with other countries under their bilateral and regional investment treaties. Thirdly, China has promoted multilateral investment rules, as demonstrated by its contributions to the G20 Guiding Principles and the WTO IFD agreement. Collectively, these developments reveal China's multifaceted role in international investment governance: it has remained a rule-taker in investment liberalization and substantive investment protection, has evolved into a rule-promoter in ISDS reform, and has emerged as a rule-maker in investment facilitation.

## References


1. Elodie Dulac (2010) The Emerging Third Generation of Chinese Investment Treaties. Transnational Dispute Settlement 4
2. United States Model BIT (2004)
3. Kenneth. J. Vandevelde (2009) A Comparison of the 2004 and 1994 U.S. Model BITs: Rebalancing Investor and Host Country Interests. In: Karl. P. Sauvant (ed), Yearbook on International Investment Law & Policy 2008–2009. Oxford, pp. 283–316
4. India Model BIT (2015)
5. White Industries Australia Limited v. The Republic of India, UNCITRAL
6. UNCTAD (2015) World Investment Report 2015: Reforming International Investment Governance. Switzerland
7. United States Model BIT (2012)
8. United States-Mexico-Canada Agreement (2018)
9. EU-Canada Comprehensive Economic and Trade Agreement (2016)
10. European Union Model BIT Clauses (2023)
11. China-Canada BIT (2012)
12. China-Japan-Korea Trilateral Investment Agreement (2012)
13. China-Tanzania BIT (2013)
14. China-Australia FTA (2015)
15. Regional Comprehensive Economic Partnership (2020)
16. UNCTAD (2020) International Investment Agreements Reform Accelerator. Switzerland
17. EU-Singapore Investment Protection Agreement (2018)
18. India-Brazil Investment Cooperation and Facilitation Treaty (2020)
19. Anthea Roberts (2017) The Shifting Landscape of Investor-State Arbitration: Loyalists, Reformists, Revolutionaries and Undecideds. Blog of the European Journal of International Law. https://www.ejiltalk.org/the-shifting-landscape-of-investor-state-arbitration-loyalists-reformists-revolutionaries-and-undecideds/. Accessed 20 August 2025
20. EU-Vietnam Investment Protection Agreement (2019)
21. UNCITRAL (2019) A/CN.9/WG.III/WP.177 Possible Reform of Investor-State Dispute Settlement (ISDS): Submission from the Government of China. https://docs.un.org/en/A/CN.9/WG.III/WP.177. Accessed 12 August 2025
22. UNCITRAL (2024) A/CN.9/WG.III/WP.249 Summary of the intersessional meeting on investor-State dispute settlement (ISDS) reform submitted by the Government of the People's Republic of China. https://docs.un.org/en/A/CN.9/WG.III/WP.249. Accessed 12 August 2025
23. Grant Hanessian and Kabir Duggal (2015) The Final 2015 Indian Model BIT: Is This Change the World Wishes to See? ICSID Review, Volume 32, Issue 1: 216–226
24. Comprehensive and Progressive Agreement for Trans-Pacific Partnership (2018)
25. G20 Guiding Principles for Global Investment Policymaking (2016)
26. UNCTAD Investment Policy Framework for Sustainable Development (2015). Switzerland
27. UNCTAD, G20 Investment Policymaking. https://investmentpolicy.unctad.org/pages/1071/g20-investment-policymaking. Accessed 20 August 2025
28. Karl P. Sauvant (2021) China Moves the G20 toward an International Investment Framework and Investment Facilitation. In: Julien Chaisse (ed) China's International Investment Strategy: Bilateral, Regional, and Global Law and Policy. Oxford, pp. 311–328.
29. UNCTAD Global Action Menu for Investment Facilitation (2016). Switzerland
30. UNCTAD, Investment Facilitation: A Review of Policy Practice (2017). Switzerland
31. OECD Policy Framework for Investment (2015). Paris
32. G20 Trade Ministers Meeting Statement (2016)
33. Axel Berger (2018) What's Next for the Investment Facilitation Agenda? Columbia FDI Perspectives No. 224. https://ccsi.columbia.edu/sites/ccsi.columbia.edu/files/content/docs/publications/No-224-Berger-FINAL.pdf. Accessed 20 August 2025

34. WTO General Council (2017) Proposal for a WTO Informal Dialogue on Investment Facilitation for Development—Joint Communication from the Friends of Investment Facilitation for Development (Job/GC/122)
35. WTO General Council (2017) Possible Elements of Investment Facilitation—Communication from China (Job/GC/123)
36. WTO General Council (2017) Possible Elements of a WTO Instrument on Investment Facilitation—Communication from Argentina and Brazil (Job/GC/124)
37. WTO General Council (2017) MIKTA Investment Workshop Reflections (Job/GC/121)
38. Junqing Chao (2019) Addressing the Global Backlash against Investment Arbitration? A Multilateral Investment Agreement and China. China and WTO Review, Volume 5, Issue 2: 269–298
39. WTO, The Investment Facilitation for Development (IFD) Agreement. https://www.wto.org/english/tratop_e/invfac_public_e/invfac_intro_e.htm. Accessed 23 August 2025
40. Zhang Xiangcheng (2017) Why Investment Facilitation Needs to be Discussed at Multilateral Level. Speech at the informal dialogues on investment facilitation (in Chinese: Wei Shen Mo Tou Zi Bian Li Hua Wen Ti Xu Yao Zai Duo Bian Tao Lun) http://chinawto.mofcom.gov.cn/article/ap/q/201706/20170602590378.shtml. Accessed 23 August 2025
41. Outlines for BRICS Investment Facilitation (2017).
42. WTO Joint Ministerial Statement on Investment Facilitation for Development (2017)
43. Investment Facilitation for Development Agreement (2024)
44. Karl P. Sauvant (2023) The New WTO Investment Facilitation for Development Agreement. Columbia FDI Perspectives, No. 363. https://ccsi.columbia.edu/sites/ccsi.columbia.edu/files/content/docs/fdi%20perspectives/No%20363%20-%20Sauvant%20-%20FINAL.pdf. Accessed 18 August 2025
45. Axel Berger (2023) China's International Investment Agreement Policy: From Rule-Taker to Rule-Maker? In: Henry Gao, Damian Raess, and Ka Zeng (ed) China and the WTO: a Twenty-Year Assessment. Cambridge, pp. 452–467
46. Freya Baetens and Sheng Zhang (2024) China: An Emerging Rule-Maker in International Investment Law? In: Ignacio de la Rasilla and Congyan Cai (ed) The Cambridge Handbook of China and International Law. Cambridge, pp. 423–449
47. China-EU Comprehensive Agreement on Investment (2020)
48. Anthea Roberts and Taylor St John (2019) UNCITRAL and ISDS Reform: China's Proposal. Blog of the European Journal of International Law. https://www.ejiltalk.org/uncitral-and-isds-reform-chinas-proposal/. Accessed 12 August 2025

# Chapter 8
# Conclusion

This chapter serves as the conclusion to the book. It begins by synthesizing the key features of and driving factors behind China's fourth-generation investment treaties (Sect. 8.1). Subsequently, it addresses these treaties within the broader context of international investment law, concluding how China and its fourth-generation investment treaties contribute to addressing the global backlash against investment arbitration and ongoing investment treaty reforms (Sect. 8.2).

## 8.1 The Emerging Fourth Generation of Chinese Investment Treaties

Chinese investment treaties, starting from 1982 to 2007, have undergone three generations and these three generations have focused on the protection of foreign investment, with its approach changing from conservative to liberal. However, since 2008, China has changed its approach to investment protection from liberal to balanced, reflecting on the global backlash against investment arbitration and learning from the US balancing practice on investment treaty making [1]. More significantly, in 2013 China accepted the pre-establishment national treatment and negative list approach under its BIT negotiations with the US [2]. This acceptance marked a breakthrough for the development of Chinese investment treaties, suggesting that they began to address both investment liberalization and protection, thereby distinguishing them from the first three generations (only focusing on investment protection). Therefore, this book argues that the fourth generation of Chinese investment treaties has emerged.

Firstly, investment liberalization is one of the most distinctive features of China's fourth-generation investment treaties. The pre-establishment national treatment and negative list approach has been officially incorporated in the 2020 RCEP and the 2020 CAI [3, 4]. For example, the RCEP provides: "[e]ach Party shall accord to investors



J. Chao, *The Emerging Fourth Generation of Chinese Investment Treaties*,
https://doi.org/10.1007/978-981-95-5052-4_8

of another Party, and to covered investments, treatment no less favourable than that it accords, in like circumstances, to its own investors and their investments *with respect to the establishment, acquisition, expansion, management, conduct, operation, and sale or other disposition of investments* in its territory." [3]

Behind this change is a fundamental liberalization of China's foreign investment regulatory regime, lasting from 2013 to 2019. In 2013, after China accepted pre-establishment national treatment during its BIT negotiations with the US, it immediately established the Shanghai FTZ to test how to reform its investment regime. At the time, China's foreign investment regulatory regime was relatively restrictive: foreign investments needed to obtain governmental approvals, were guided by the Guidance Catalogue, and were mainly regulated by a special framework of "Three Foreign Investment Laws". Considering this, the Shanghai FTZ replaced the approval system with the recordation system and formulated the negative list for special administrative measures [5, 6]. These practices were successful and subsequently introduced to other FTZs and nationwide [7].

Moreover, the New Foreign Investment Law was approved in 2019, aiming to replace the "Three Foreign Investment Laws" and establish a new, open, and liberalized foreign investment regulatory regime. The New Foreign Investment Law expressly provides that China "*applies the administrative system of pre-establishment national treatment plus negative list to foreign investment*", and that outside the negative list, foreign investment administration shall be implemented "*under the principle of equal treatment for domestic and foreign investment*" [8]. Furthermore, the New Foreign Investment Law establishes an information reporting system and a national security review mechanism for better management of foreign investment [8].

In addition to the pre-establishment national treatment and negative list approach, China's fourth-generation investment treaties have addressed other liberalization issues, including absolute market access obligations, SOE disciplines, performance requirement prohibitions, regulatory transparency, environmental protection, labor rights, corporate social responsibility, climate change as well as investment facilitation [3, 4]. Compared with the US BITs, EU FTAs and recent mega-regional agreements (including the 2016 CETA, 2018 USMCA, and 2018 CPTPP), China's fourth-generation investment treaties have undertaken substantial and comprehensive commitments in each of these critical areas [3, 4, 9–13]. These treaty commitments demonstrate China's determination to create a fairer, more open, and more transparent investment environment.

Secondly, investment protection remains as a central issue for China's fourth-generation investment treaties, but the approach has shifted from liberal to balanced, aligning with current trends in investment treaty reform. This balancing practice has been undertaken between investment protection and the right of states to regulate for legitimate public policy objectives. On the substantive level, the meanings of key provisions have been clarified to prevent arbitral tribunals from adopting expansive interpretations, while new exception clauses have been incorporated to safeguard the regulatory space of host states. The details are as follows:

(1) Definition of investment: two methods have been adopted to refine the previous broad definition: (a) requiring investments to fulfill certain characteristics, and (b) explicitly excluding certain types of assets from investment definition [13 –17]. These two methods aim to codify the exiting arbitral jurisprudence and address long-standing controversies in arbitral practice [14].
(2) Definition of investor: additional requirements have been introduced for legal entities—requiring them to engage in substantial business activities in host states—to exclude shell companies from the coverage of investment treaties [3, 14, 16]. Furthermore, some post-2008 Chinese investment treaties have explicitly included SOEs in the investor definition [18]. This explicit inclusion may help mitigate potential risks in investment arbitration cases brought by Chinese SOEs,.
(3) National treatment and MFN treatment: most post-2008 Chinese investment treaties have explicitly provided that national treatment and MFN treatment should be granted in "like circumstances" [3, 15–17, 19]. Furthermore, these treaties have clarified that MFN treatment does not encompass any international dispute resolution procedures [3, 15–17, 19].
(4) FET and FPS standards: most post-2008 Chinese investment treaties have adopted the non-exhaustive list approach to clarify the scope of FET and FPS standards. The non-exhaustive list approach typically encompasses three key clarifications: (a) establishing customary international law as the ceiling to the FET and FPS standards; (b) providing a non-exclusive list of examples for the meaning of FET and FPS standards; and (c) stipulating that a violation of other provisions does not automatically constitute a violation of FET and FPS obligations [3, 15–17, 19]. A closer examination of these post-2008 treaties reveals that they have largely incorporated the second and third clarifications while demonstrating inconsistency and hesitancy to the first [3, 15–17, 19–22].
(5) Indirect expropriation: most post-2008 Chinese investment treaties have introduced an annex defining and clarifying indirect expropriation. Notably, they have listed the factors tribunals should consider when determining indirect expropriation, including the economic impact of measures, interference with reasonable investment-backed expectations, and the character of measures [3, 15–17, 19]. Furthermore, they have introduced an expropriation exception for nondiscriminatory regulatory measures adopted to achieve legitimate public policy objectives [3, 15–17, 19].
(6) Exception clauses: most post-2008 Chinese investment treaties have incorporated new exception clauses to safeguard the regulatory space of host states in the areas such as essential security, environmental protection, prudential and monetary policy [15].

Overall, China's fourth-generation investment treaties have largely established a balanced approach to substantive provisions. However, two critical issues require attention: (1) the explicit inclusion of SOEs under the definition of investor; and (2) the treatment of investors' legitimate expectations under the FET standard. Moreover, China should consistently maintain this balancing approach in its future treaty practice. Through such measures, these fourth-generation investment treaties can more effectively achieve the balance between investment protection and the right of states to regulate.

On the procedural level, during the period from 2008 to 2015, China's fourth-generation investment treaties progressively refined ISDS provisions for promoting a more comprehensive and balanced mechanism [15–17, 19]. For example, the 2012 China-Canada BIT enhances the ISDS mechanism in three key aspects:

(1) the treaty establishes a two-step procedure: "consultation and negotiation + submission" and imposes "six months + three years" imitation periods for the submission of claims [15];
(2) the treaty enhances contracting parties' engagement in arbitral proceedings through the participation of non-disputing contracting party, the binding treaty interpretation by the contracting parties and so forth. To improve the fairness and efficiency of the ISDS mechanism, some other issues are addressed concerning claim consolidation, third party, arbitrators, and arbitral transparency [15];
(3) the treaty stipulates that final awards may only impose monetary damage and applicable interests, aiming to preserve contracting states' regulatory autonomy while ensuring compensation for affected investors [15].

After 2015, following the intensifying global debates on ISDS and the emergence of divergent reform proposals, China has fundamentally reconsidered and reassessed the existing ISDS mechanism. In 2019, China submitted its proposal for ISDS reform at UNCITRAL Working Group III. The proposal advocated for the establishment of a permanent multilateral appellate mechanism, while simultaneously integrating this appellate mechanism with the current investment arbitration system [23]. A closer examination shows that the hybrid approach in China's ISDS reform proposal was primarily rooted in its domestic arbitration practice, diverging from conventional understanding of international arbitration. This distinction may explain why some international scholars expressed confusion when the approach was first introduced [24].

Given these considerations, China's policymakers are advised to engage in substantive discussions with Chinese companies and lawyers who have actively participated in investment arbitration in recent years. In fact, in October 2024, China hosted an UNCITRAL intersessional meeting in Chengdu to discuss the key issues of the appellate mechanism [25]. It is believed that these discussions can help China formulate more widely accepted ISDS reform proposals and contribute to establishing an international consensus on a more effective and predictable ISDS mechanism.

Moreover, China's fourth-generation investment treaties are advised to clarify their applicability to the Hong Kong and Macao SARs. As discussed, China's post-handover agreements with Britain and Portugal has established that these treaties do not automatically extend to the Hong Kong and Macao SARs unless the Chinese Central government—after consulting the views of SAR governments—explicitly determines otherwise [26]. Yet, this principle has been misunderstood in China's investment arbitration cases, as evidenced by *Sanum Investments v. Laos,* causing legal uncertainty [27, 28, 29]. Consequently, the new treaties should explicitly codify this policy to prevent future disputes.

To conclude, China's fourth-generation investment treaties reflect a liberal approach to investment liberalization and a balanced approach to investment protection. To date, these treaties have undertaken substantial liberalization commitments and established balanced substantive protection provisions. However, certain challenges remain—particularly concerning ISDS reform. Overall, compared to the first three generations, the fourth generation's key features have been summarized in Table 8.1 as below.

The emergence of China's fourth-generation investment treaties can be contributed to five key factors:

(1) The evolving landscape of international investment treaties has shifted over the past two decades, with their focus expanding from pure investment protection to encompassing protection, liberalization and facilitation.
(2) The global backlash against investment arbitration has created an international consensus that investment treaties should preserve the regulatory space of host states for legitimate public policy objectives, requiring a balance between investment protection and the right to regulate.
(3) China's fundamental liberalization reforms in its foreign investment regulatory regime, particularly through the 2019 New Foreign Investment Law, have established a more open framework that enables comprehensive commitments on investment liberalization.
(4) China's growing ODFI, particularly driven by the BRI, has transformed its role from primarily a capital importer to both an importer and exporter, fundamentally reshaping its approach to investment treaties.
(5) China's increasing involvement in international arbitration over the past five years has provided practical insights that are influencing its fourth-generation treaty practice, while positioning China to play a more proactive role in global investment regime reform.

It should be noted that these five factors are dynamic and constantly evolving. These features explain why the fourth generation's development represents a gradual and ongoing process—contrasting with the clear turning points that characterized the first three generations. More significantly, these dynamic and constantly evolving factors will continue to shape China's approach to remaining challenges and its ultimate stance on fourth-generation treaty practice.

**Table 8.1** Key Characteristics of China's Four Generations of Investment Treaties

| | 1st G | 2nd G | 3rd G | 4th G |
|---|---|---|---|---|
| Period | 1982–1989 | 1990–1997 | 1998–2007 | 2008-present |
| Protection | Conservative | Conservative | Liberal | Balanced |
| Liberalization | Not Addressed | | | Liberal |

## 8.2 Global Backlash Against Investment Arbitration, Investment Treaty Reform and China

As discussed, there is currently a global backlash against investment arbitration. The criticisms initially stemmed from arbitral tribunals' expansive interpretations of investment treaty provisions, later expanding to include concerns over inconsistency of awards, bias of arbitrators, lack of regulations governing investors and so forth [30]. More significantly, questions arose as to whether the current international investment regime unduly constrained host states' regulatory space for legitimate public policy objectives. In response, Bolivia, Ecuador, and Venezuela withdrew from the ICSID Convention, Indonesia and South Africa terminated their investment treaties and Australia declined to include ISDS provisions in future treaties [31]. Beyond these radical reactions, most states—including the US, the EU, China, and India—have reformulated their investment treaties to strike a balance between investment protection and the right of states to regulate.

China's fourth-generation investment treaties serve as its balancing model. A closer examination of the specific balanced provisions of China, the US, the EU, and India reveals that while all four states have explicitly reaffirmed the right of states to regulate in their treaty preambles, they have differed in how they operationalize this principle through specific balanced provisions [3, 9–12, 15–17, 32]. Key challenges include the clarification of FET and FPS standards and the ISDS reform. Additionally, other balanced provisions—including definitions of investment and investor, national treatment and MFN treatment, indirect expropriation, and exception clauses—exhibit subtle but significant variations [3, 9–12, 15–17, 32].

As discussed in Chap. 7, in the balancing debate, the US, the EU, and India have primarily drawn on their experiences in investment arbitration, whereas China has largely learned from the US experience and the global best practices in investment treaty reform. This is partly because China has only began actively participating in investment arbitration in recent years. Consequently, it may be premature to claim that China's fourth-generation investment treaties will significantly influence national-level investment treaty reforms. However, China's learning process could contribute to the consolidation of investment treaty rules.

Beyond the national level, investment treaty reforms have also progressed at the bilateral, regional and multilateral levels [33]. Bilaterally and regionally, a large number of investment agreements have been negotiated and concluded, offering states an opportunity to collectively review and refine reform efforts [33]. Notably, these agreements—particularly mega-regional ones—have the potential to lead to the consolidation of investment treaty rules [33]. For example, China concluded the RCEP in 2020 and formally applied to the CPTPP in 2021.

A closer comparison of the CPTPP and RCEP reveals significant convergence in substantive balanced provisions, including their preambles, definitions of investment and investor, national treatment, MFN treatment, FET and FPS standards, indirect expropriation, and exception clauses [3, 13]. This convergence suggests that these treaties could play a significant role in fostering treaty consolidation. Moreover, it provides a solid foundation for the OECD's ongoing moderation efforts in this field [34]. The core challenge, however, remains ISDS reform. As discussed, in 2017, UNCITRAL established Working Group III to focus specifically on ISDS reform. To date, Working Group III has achieved some outcomes in terms of individual reforms, such as promoting mediation and establishing advisory centers, and is now pursuing a more ambitious initiative, creating a standing mechanism with an appellate mechanism [35–38]. As discussed, China has actively participated in UNCITRAL reform efforts, as evidenced by its ISDS reform proposal.

At the multilateral levels, in addition to OECD and UNCITRAL, China has actively promoted investment rulemaking through the G20 and WTO. Specifically, the 2016 G20 under China's presidency concluded the G20 Guiding Principles [39]. Although these non-binding principles were criticized as being "too general", they represented the first multilateral consensus on investment issues "reached between a varied group of developed, developing and transition economies"—a milestone highlighted by the UNCTAD [40]. More significantly, the 2016 G20 Summit initiated discussions on investment facilitation [41]. While no concrete outcomes were achieved at the time, these discussions laid the groundwork for future progress on the issue.

Following these developments, in 2017 China joined other states in proposing investment facilitation discussions at the WTO [42]. Meanwhile, China submitted its Investment Facilitation Communication for WTO Members' consideration [43]. These efforts ultimately led to the finalization of the WTO IFD agreement in 2024 [44]. A closer examination reveals that the WTO IFD agreement and China's Investment Facilitation Communication exhibit substantial overlaps, particularly in three critical areas: (1) enhanced regulatory transparency, (2) streamlined administrative procedures, and (3) special and differential treatment for developing and least-developed countries [43, 44].

Finally, China's evolving role in international investment governance should be analyzed through the lens of four key dimensions in its fourth-generation investment treaties. Specifically:

(1) *Rule-taker in investment liberalization and substantive protection*: China has primarily followed established norms in these filed. As discussed, China's comprehensive liberalization commitments have been significantly influenced through its treaty negations with the US and the EU and complemented by its own comprehensive reforms to its foreign investment regulatory framework. In striking a substantive balance between investment protection and the right of states to regulate, China has primarily learned from US experience and the global best practices in investment treaty reform.
(2) *Rule-promoter in ISDS Reform*: China has transitioned to an active role in ongoing ISDS reform, notably through its proposal submitted to UNCITRAL in 2019 [23]. However, as discussed, China's proposal—largely built upon its domestic arbitration system—differed from the conventional perception of international arbitration. In 2024, China hosted an UNCITRAL intersessional meeting in Chengdu to discuss the key issues of the appellate mechanism [25].

Considering these developments, China is more appropriately characterized as a rule-promoter rather than a rule-maker in ISDS reform.

(3) *Rule-maker in Investment Facilitation*: China has established itself as a leader in investment facilitation rulemaking, demonstrated by its proactive advancement of discussions and substantial textual inputs at both the G20 and WTO [41–44].

Overall, China's fourth-generation investment treaties have largely taken shape. Compared with the first three generations, their defining characteristics lie in promoting investment liberalization while balancing investment protection with the right of states to regulate. Amid the global backlash against investment arbitration and ongoing investment treaty reforms, the emergence of China's fourth-generation investment treaties serves as a stabilizing force for the international investment regime. As both a major capital-importing and exporting country, China has chosen not to abandon the system outright, but instead has proactively sought balanced approaches to reform the system. Moreover, in emerging areas such as investment liberalization and facilitation, China has demonstrated a willingness to make extensive treaty commitments, comprehensively advance domestic regulatory liberalization, and actively promote global discussions to reach consensus. Therefore, within the evolving international investment landscape, China and its fourth-generation investment treaties have played a significant role and made substantive contributions to the regime's development.

## References


1. Elodie Dulac (2010) The Emerging Third Generation of Chinese Investment Treaties. Transnational Dispute Settlement 4
2. U.S. Department of the Treasury (2013) Joint U.S.-China Economic Track Fact Sheet of the Fifth Meeting of the U.S.-China Strategic and Economic Dialogue. https://home.treasury.gov/news/press-releases/jl2010Accessed 7 August 2025. Accessed 7 August 2025
3. Regional Comprehensive Economic Partnership (2020)
4. China-EU Comprehensive Agreement on Investment (2020)
5. Notice of the Shanghai Municipal People's Government on Issuing the Measures for the Recordation Administration of Foreign-Funded Enterprises in China (Shanghai) Pilot Free Trade Zone (2013)
6. Notice of the Shanghai Municipal People's Government on Issuing the Measures for the Recordation Administration of Foreign-Funded Projects in China (Shanghai) Pilot Free Trade Zone (2013)
7. Notice of the General Office of the State Council on Issuing the Special Management Measures (Negative List) for Foreign Investment Access in Pilot Free Trade Zones (2015)
8. Foreign Investment Law of the People's Republic of China (2019)
9. United States Model BIT (2004)
10. United States Model BIT (2012)
11. EU-Canada Comprehensive Economic and Trade Agreement (2016)
12. United States-Mexico-Canada Agreement (2018)
13. Comprehensive and Progressive Agreement for Trans-Pacific Partnership (2018)
14. UNCTAD (2020) International Investment Agreements Reform Accelerator. Switzerland
15. China-Canada BIT (2012)

16. China-Australia FTA (2015)
17. China-Japan-Korea Trilateral Investment Agreement (2012)
18. China-Mexico BIT (2008)
19. China-Korea FTA (2015)
20. China-ASEAN Investment Agreement (2009)
21. China-Peru FTA (2009)
22. China-New Zealand FTA (2008)
23. UNCITRAL (2019) A/CN.9/WG.III/WP.177 Possible Reform of Investor-State Dispute Settlement (ISDS): Submission from the Government of China. https://docs.un.org/en/A/CN.9/WG.III/WP.177. Accessed 12 August 2025
24. Anthea Roberts and Taylor St John (2019) UNCITRAL and ISDS Reform: China's Proposal. Blog of the European Journal of International Law. https://www.ejiltalk.org/uncitral-and-isds-reform-chinas-proposal/. Accessed 12 August 2025
25. UNCITRAL (2024) A/CN.9/WG.III/WP.249 Summary of the intersessional meeting on investor-State dispute settlement (ISDS) reform submitted by the Government of the People's Republic of China. https://docs.un.org/en/A/CN.9/WG.III/WP.249. Accessed 12 August 2025
26. Hong Xu (2016) The Application of International Treaties to the Hong Kong and Macao Special Administrative Regions. Legal Daily (in Chinese: Guo Ji Tiao Yue Shi Yong Xiang Gang He Ao Men Te Qu De Shi Jian).
27. Sanum Investments v. Lao People's Democratic Republic, PCA Case No. 2013–13, Award on Jurisdiction (13 December 2013)
28. Sanum Investments v. Lao People's Democratic Republic, Judgment of the High Court of Singapore [2015] SGHC 15 (20 January 2015)
29. Sanum Investments v. Lao People's Democratic Republic, Judgment of the Court of Appeal of Singapore [2016] SGCA 57 (29 September 2016)
30. 31. Michael Waibel, Asha Kaushal, Kyo-Hwa Liz Chung and Claire Balchin (eds) (2010) The Backlash against Investment Arbitration. Kluwer, London
31. Chin Leng Lim (2020) Reaching for Utopia, Geneva as Inspiration for Investment Disputes?. In: Meredith Kolsky Lewis, Junji Nakagawa, Rostam J. Neuwirth, Colin B. Picker, and Peter-Tobias Stoll (ed) A Post-WTO International Legal Order Utopian, Dystopian and Other Scenarios. Springer, Switzerland, p 167–185
32. India Model BIT (2015)
33. UNCTAD (2015) World Investment Report 2015: Reforming International Investment Governance. Switzerland
34. OECD, Modernising investment treaties (Track 2). https://www.oecd.org/en/topics/sub-issues/the-future-of-investment-treaties/modernising-investment-treaties.html. Accessed 18 August 2025
35. Anthea Roberts and Taylor St John (2023) UNCITRAL and ISDS Reform: Moving to the Delivery Phase. Blog of the European Journal of International Law. https://www.ejiltalk.org/uncitral-and-isds-reform-moving-to-the-delivery-phase/. Accessed 11 August 2025
36. UNCITRAL (2024) UNCITRAL Working Group III Concludes Its Work on the Draft Statute of an Advisory Centre on International Investment Dispute Resolution. https://unis.unvienna.org/unis/pressrels/2024/unisl355.html. Accessed 18 August 2025
37. UNCITRAL Working Group III (2024) A/CN.9/WG.III/WP.239 - Possible reform of investor-State dispute settlement (ISDS): Draft statute of a standing mechanism for the resolution of international investment disputes. https://docs.un.org/en/A/CN.9/WG.III/WP.239. Accessed 11 August 2025
38. UNCITRAL Working Group III (2025) A/CN.9/WG.III/WP.256 - Possible reform of investor-State dispute settlement (ISDS): Structure and design of a standing mechanism for the resolution of international investment disputes. https://docs.un.org/en/A/CN.9/WG.III/WP.256. Accessed 11 August 2025
39. G20 Guiding Principles for Global Investment Policymaking (2016)
40. UNCTAD, G20 Investment Policymaking. https://investmentpolicy.unctad.org/pages/1071/g20-investment-policymaking. Accessed 20 August 2025

41. Karl P. Sauvant (2021) China Moves the G20 toward an International Investment Framework and Investment Facilitation. In: Julien Chaisse (ed) China's International Investment Strategy: Bilateral, Regional, and Global Law and Policy. Oxford, p 311–328.
42. WTO General Council (2017) Proposal for a WTO Informal Dialogue on Investment Facilitation for Development - Joint Communication from the Friends of Investment Facilitation for Development (Job/GC/122)
43. WTO General Council (2017) Possible Elements of Investment Facilitation - Communication from China (Job/GC/123)
44. IFD agreement Investment Facilitation for Development Agreement (2024)

MIX
Papier aus verantwortungsvollen Quellen
Paper from responsible sources
FSC® C105338

If you have any concerns about our products,
you can contact us on
**ProductSafety@springernature.com**

In case Publisher is established outside the EU,
the EU authorized representative is:
**Springer Nature Customer Service Center GmbH**
**Europaplatz 3, 69115 Heidelberg, Germany**

Printed by Libri Plureos GmbH
in Hamburg, Germany